ISRAEL

𝔹B BONECHI

STEIMATZKY

STEIMATZKY MEANS BOOKS

© Copyright
by Casa Editrice Bonechi, via Cairoli 18/b, Firenze - Italia
E-mail: bonechi@bonechi.it

Concept and project: Casa Editrice Bonechi.
Editorial management: Monica Bonechi.
Graphic design, layout and cover: Manuela Ranfagni.
Texts: Rita Bianucci, Giovanna Magi and Giuliano Valdes
– Editing Studio, Pisa. Editing: Elena Rossi.
Map: Stefano Benini.

Printed in Italy by Centro Stampa Editoriale Bonechi,
Sesto Fiorentino.

The photographs in this book are the property of the
Casa Editrice Bonechi Archives and were taken by Paolo
Giambone, Andrea Innocenti, Garo Nalbandian, Sandra
Papi, Andrea Pistolesi, and Alessandro Saragosa.

The following photographers also contributed
to this publication:
Israel Museum/David Harris – Jerusalem (p. 41 bottom);
Photo Mendrea (p. 1 top and bottom left, 3 bottom, 4, 5,
6, 7, 8 left, 14, 15, 16 bottom, 34 top, 35, 37 bottom right,
38 bottom, 39 bottom, 42, 43, 46-47 top, 48 top, 51 top
right, 52, 53, 54-55 bottom, 55, 56, 57, 59, 60, 61, 62-63,
65, 66, 67, 72-73, 79, 81 top, 82, 83, 84, 85 top, 86, 87,
88-89 top, 89 bottom, 90, 91, 92 top, 93, 94, 96, 98-99,
99 top, 100, 101, 102, 103, 104, 105 top and bottom right,
106-107 top, 107, 108, 109, 110, 111, 112, 113, 114, 115,
116, 117, 118, 119, 120 top, 122-123, 124, 125, 126-127).

The publisher apologizes for any unintentional
omissions, and would be pleased to include appropriate
acknowledgements in any subsequent edition
of this publication.

ISBN 978-88-476-2559-4
www.bonechi.com

TABLE OF CONTENTS

Introduction

Silybum marianum (L.) Gaertner, *a spiny herbaceous annual typical of the fields in the Mediterranean region. Israel's flora counts a great number of species, thanks in part to the marked climatic differences from area to area.*

Bottom, a view of the ruins of Masada, a site with a marvelous vista of the Dead Sea.

Israel is a small country in the Near East that stretches from the Mediterranean to the deserts of Syria and Arabia. The territory is divided into three natural regions: the coastal area, the mountains, and the tectonic rift that is the bed of the country's major watercourse, the River Jordan. The coastland is a fertile and well-watered plain; it is densely populated (and the site of large cities such as Tel Aviv and Haifa) and is served by important communications routes. The mountainous region occupies the center of the country, extending from Lebanon in the north to the Gulf of Eilat (or Aqaba) in the south. Some of Israel's highest mountains are located here: Mount Meron (1208 m), Mount Ba'al Hatsor (1016 m), and Mount Ramon (1037 m). Finally, the Jordan Rift Valley marks a portion of Israel's eastern border. The area includes two lakes, the Sea of Galilee and the Dead Sea, the salt lake at the Earth's lowest elevation on dry land (413 m below sea level). The Golan Heights, a broad plateau and mountainous region, runs from the northeastern corner of Israeli territory into Syria, where most of the formation lies. Israel's highest peak is on the Heights: Mount Hermon (2224 m). The southern portion of the country, the Negev region, is mostly desert. Thanks to the variety of its landscapes and climatic diversities, Israel attracts tourists of all kinds. The country's long and varied history has made it a meeting point for various cultures, ethnicities, and religions. Thousands of pilgrims travel each year to the churches, the synagogues, and the resplendent mosques of Jerusalem and other Israeli cities. The fascinating archaeological sites scattered throughout the territory have something for every aficionado of ancient art and history. The many different natural beauty spots and the magnificent natural parks enchant nature lovers and invite open-air adventures: Israel hosts upwards of two thousand species of flora, many of which are autochthonous; the abundant fauna is well represented by mammal, reptile, bird, and insect species. Rural tourism has grown by leaps and bounds in recent years; visitors can choose between stays at the kibbutzim so typical of the country or at the moshavim or in small villages: all new ways of learning about the country and spending vacation time in contact with nature, far from chaotic urban rhythms. Israel is also a perfect destination for visitors whose uppermost priority is relaxation and wellbeing: the Dead Sea and the Sea of Galilee areas are world-renowned for their excellent spa centers. And finally, Israel is a center for business tourism: the country vaunts an advanced economy and well-entrenched industry and is at the avant-garde in many sectors, including communications, defense, and medicine.

HISTORY THROUGH THE MILLENNIA

From Prehistory to the Roman Conquest

The first settlements in what is now Israel date to the area's Middle Paleolithic age (about 120,000 - 36,000 years ago). Archaeological digs have proven that the territory was inhabited by Canaanite tribes at least until the mid-second millennium BCE, when populations of Semitic origin migrated to the region, the Israelites taking up residence in the hilly regions of the interior. Originally divided into twelve tribes, this people was united in the late 2nd millennium BCE by Saul, the first King of Israel. Saul's successor David enlarged the kingdom and made Jerusalem its capital. At the dawn of the 1st millennium BCE, David's son Solomon built the First Temple in Jerusalem to house the Ark of the Covenant. After Solomon's death, the territory was divided into two kingdoms: Israel, which united the ten northern tribes, and Judah, populated by the remaining two tribes and located on the hills around Jerusalem. The Kingdom of Israel was conquered by the Assyrians in 721 BCE. The Kingdom of Judah was seized by the Babylonians in 586 BCE; the Jewish population was deported to Babylon. Solomon's Temple was demolished. In 539 BCE, Babylon was conquered by the Persians and the Jews were permitted to return to Jerusalem; the Second Temple was built. Over the succeeding centuries, the land and its people were repeatedly conquered by outside forces: the Macedonian Greeks under Alexander, the Ptolomeic Egyptians, the Seleucids, and the Hasmoneans, who reigned until the Romans took control of the entire area in 63 BCE.

From Roman Times to the 19th Century

The Israeli territory was part of the Roman empire for about two centuries. Roman domination bred unrest, which culminated in the Great Jewish Revolt of 66-70 CE: Emperor Titus succeeded in quelling the revolt; his troops also destroyed Jerusalem and its Temple and deported thousands of Jews to Rome. Bar Kokhba led another rebellion against the Romans in 131 CE; this revolt was put down by Emperor Hadrian, who renamed Jerusalem *Aelia Capitolina* and made the territory a Roman province, Syria Palaestina. In the 4th century, when the Roman empire was already divided by internal strife, Palestine was annexed to the Eastern Roman Empire and remained under Byzantine control until the 7th century. Much of the area was Christianized

On this page: top, the remains of "Solomon's Gate" (10th c. BCE) at Gezer; bottom, inside the archaeological area, the row of stelae that may have been part of a Canaanite temple, dating to 1600 BCE ca.

Facing page: top, a view of the Judean desert; center, a Bedouin woman driving her flock to pasture; bottom, a detail of the frieze in the ancient synagogue at Capernaum (4th c. CE).

in this period. But in 638, Arabs led by Caliph Omar conquered Palestine. Moslem Arab rule lasted for four centuries and was a period of relative peace for the region. In the 11th century the area was thrown into confusion by the Crusades: led by Godefroy de Bouillon, Crusader troops took control of Jerusalem in 1099 and in 1100 founded the first of the Crusader states, the Kingdom of Jerusalem. This state of affairs persisted until 1187, when the Moslems regained control of the area. The ensuing Ottoman period was marked by alternating moments of great prosperity (for example, under Suleiman the Magnificent in the 16th century) and others of great decadence. Jewish immigration from other areas to what is now the State of Israel began in the 19th century: the first to arrive were Russians, who founded a farming colony near Jaffa (1882); they were followed by massive inflows of immigrants from Eastern Europe.

The Early 1900s and the Two World Wars
The objectives of the Zionist movement, founded in 1897, were to encourage the return of the Jews to Palestine and to create a Jewish political entity. The Jewish National Fund was established in 1901 for the purpose of purchasing land for Jewish settlement; the first kibbutz was founded at Degania in 1909. The Ottoman empire fell during World War I: in 1917, English troops occupied Jerusalem and the Palestinian territory, and in the same year, Great Britain approved the Balfour Declaration stating that Britain "viewed with favor the establishment in Palestine of a national home for the Jewish people." The document was violently opposed by the Arabs and there began a series of conflicts between the two sides – which nevertheless little discouraged Jewish immigration. In 1922, the League of Nations granted Great Britain the Palestine Mandate: Britain proposed subdividing the territory into two states, one Arab and one Jewish, but the project was not approved. 1933 saw an increase of Jewish immigration to Palestine (due in large part to persecution by the Nazi regime); in 1939, Great Britain published the White Paper, the aim of which was to drastically limit the flow of immigrants; in actual practice,

it only encouraged development of an "underground railroad" and immigration increased considerably during World War II. After 6 million Jews had been exterminated in the concentration camps during the Holocaust, immigration increased again in the immediate postwar period. In 1947, Great Britain requested that its Mandate be placed on the United Nations agenda: a special commission recommended that the area west of the River Jordan be partitioned into two states (one Arab, one Jewish) and that Jerusalem be placed under international protection. This proposal was rejected by the Arab leaders, a fact that only heightened the tensions between the two sides. Britain's Mandate over Palestine expired on 15 May 1948; on 14 May, the Jewish community in Palestine proclaimed the State of Israel.

The State of Israel

On 15 May 1948, Egyptian, Jordanian, Syrian, Iraqi, and Saudi armies invaded the newborn State of Israel: many Arabs fled or were expelled from the territory and were moved to refugee camps with the promise that they could return to their homes at the end of the conflict. The armistice agreements that ended the 1948 Arab-Israeli War (1949) granted Galilee and the Negev to Israel, the West Bank (Judea and Samaria) to Jordan, and the Gaza Strip to Egypt. Jerusalem was split down the middle, with the eastern area, comprising the Old City, going to Jordan and the western side, with the new city, to Israel. With the Law of Return, enacted in 1950 following the conflict, Israel opened its borders to all Jews wishing to return to the land of their forebears but denied reentry to Arab refugees. During the 1950s, Israel engaged another war with Egypt for control of the Suez Canal: after the Canal was nationalized by Egypt in 1956, Israel attacked and succeeded in seizing the Gaza Strip and the Sinai Peninsula, territories which were returned to Egypt in 1957. But tension in this area of the Middle East did not abate and in fact escalated, culminating in the Six Day War of 1967, fought on three fronts: Egyptian, Jordanian, and Syrian. The conflict won Israel control of the Sinai Peninsula, the West Bank, the Golan Heights, and East Jerusalem, reuniting the city. The 1970s opened with the Yom Kippur War in 1973, when Syrian and Egyptian forces launched a joint attack on Israel. After three weeks of conflict, the Israelis had penetrated into Africa and toward Damascus. The agreements reached thanks in part to mediation by U.S. Secretary of State Henry Kissinger were the basis for the peace treaty with Egypt, which stipulated Egyptian recognition of Israel as an independent state and Israeli withdrawal of troops from all the Egyptian territories occupied in 1967. Israel returned to war in 1982, this time against a Palestinian enclave in southern Lebanon: the Israeli army advanced into Lebanese territory as far as Beirut but withdrew three years later, maintaining control only of a security buffer zone along the bor-

On this page: a capital from the Byzantine church excavated at Kursi (5th-6th c. CE); bottom, a detail of the floor mosaic, depicting the god Apollo, found at Hammat Tiberias.

Facing page: top, one of the spectacular grottos at the Rosh Hanikra nature reserve, north of Haifa; bottom, a view of the Temple Esplanade in Jerusalem.

ISRAEL'S ARCHAEOLOGICAL SITES

The map of Israel is dotted with archeological sites referred to a period from extending from prehistoric times through the Ottoman (Turkish-Islamic) era. Interest in archaeology in Israel began in the late 19th / early 20th century, when the Jewish Palestine Exploration Society was founded. Israel's archaeological heritage creates a strong bond between the country's past and present, revealing hands-on history and casting new light on the cultures, social structures, and daily lies of the many peoples who have inhabited this land over the millennia. Many of Israel's archeological sites are now protected by the UNESCO World Heritage program. Of particular note, the remains of the Canaanite cities of **Tel Hazor**, **Megiddo** (with finds that range from the Chalcolithic period to the era of Persian rule), **Beersheba**, the Nabatean cities of **Mamshit**, **Haluza**, **Avdat**, and **Shivta** in the Negev, Herod's fortress at **Masada**, and the **Citadel** of Akko, with its Crusader-era ruins.

THE KIBBUTZIM

The kibbutz is a collective community typical of Israel, based on egalitarian principles and the concept of common ownership. The first kibbutz was founded in 1909 at Degania on the shores of the Sea of Galilee. These communities live by agriculture; the members receive no salaries but shared all the village structures and services. The kibbutzim were extremely important in the history of the State of Israel: they formed its skeleton and played a determinant role in formation of Israeli society. Today, although their number is dwindling, Israel still counts about 270 kibbutzim that engage not only in agriculture but, recently, also in manufacturing and industry, notably in the plastics and electronics sectors. Many of the kibbutzim have also discovered a vocation for tourism, opening hotels or bed and breakfast establishments, craft shops, and offering numerous other tourist services.

der. The widespread Palestinian popular uprising of 1987 marked the start of what is known as the First Intifada; it continued until 1993, when Yasser Arafat (Chairman of the PLO – Palestine Liberation Organization – founded in 1964) and Shimon Peres signed the Oslo Accords by which Palestinians and Israelis agreed to mutual recognition, renouncing terrorism and other violence. Arafat was permitted to again enter Gaza and the West Bank in 1994. Ratification of the second round of the Accords created the Palestinian National Authority. The 21st century opened with a Second Intifada; that is, another Palestinian revolt sparked by what was felt to be a "provocatory" visit by Ariel Sharon to the Temple Esplanade. A new series of rioting and clashes fanned the Israeli-Palestinian conflict: the violence lost momentum only after the death of Yasser Arafat in 2004. Tensions between Israel and Lebanon flared up again in 2006: after the Hezbollah launched missiles against several Israeli cities, Israel mounted an offensive against Lebanon to wipe out the armed faction of the party. After the UN ceasefire, a peacekeeping force was sent to southern Lebanon with the aim of disarming the Hezbollah, securing the border, and overseeing withdrawal of the Israeli troops.

Jerusalem

Jerusalem is a treasure trove of archaeology, religion, and art. Over the course of its history, the city has been razed and rebuilt scores of times. Its importance derives not so much from its geographical position as from the fact that it is the holy city of the world's three major monotheistic religions: Jerusalem is home to the Holy Sepulchre of Christ, venerated by Christians, the Rock from which Mohammed ascended, sacred to Muslims, and the Western (or Wailing) Wall, a place of worship for those of the Jewish faith. The heart of Jerusalem is without a doubt the Old City with its four quarters (Jewish, Muslim, Christian, and Armenian), dominated by the Temple Esplanade, and narrow streets and colorful markets crowded with tourists and pilgrims. The new city (built up beginning in the mid-19th century) is starkly modern in contrast, with skyscrapers, shopping malls, and striking works of engineering: a hymn to the continuing vitality of an ancient city that is still growing.

The Chords Bridge by the Spanish architect Santiago Calatrava. Bottom right, a panorama of Jerusalem. Facing page: top, a view of the Mamilla district.

Citadel and Tower of David

Situated next to Jaffa Gate, the **Citadel** encompasses an area where once stood three towers built by King Herod: the Phasael Tower (named for his brother), Hippicus Tower (named for his friend) and the Miriamne Tower (named for his wife). They were to guard Herod's adjacent palace and were later spared destruction by Titus' Roman army in order to house his Twelfth

One view of excavations inside the Citadel, with the arch from the Mamluk period, and the minaret known as the Tower of David.

Legion. During the Byzantine era, it was in such a state of ruin that philosophers and recluses chose it as a place of meditation. It was used as a fortress headquarters in the 12th century by the Crusaders, who repaired its walls and surrounded it by a moat. The Muslim Mamluks demolished it in 1239 and it remained in a state of abandon until 1335 when the Turks repaired its walls and added the minaret known today as the **Tower of David.** The Citadel became a British base during the Mandate (1917-1948) and then a Jordanian one until 1967. Today, it houses the **Museum of the History of Jerusalem** and is famous for the sound and light shows presented on its walls.

One of the bastions of the fortifications.

CARDO

A few meters beneath the level of the existing road is the **Cardo Maximus**, the route that led from the Damascus Gate to the old Zion Gate which was located a little farther from the Zion Gate we see today. The road dates from the period of the *Aelia Capitolina*, yet its current features are from the Byzantine era when major restorations and building work were done.

The Cardo was a broad, colonnaded street, flanked by porticoes and shops. The part we can see today, with its columns and Corinthian capitals is about half as wide as the original.

Three images of the area of the Cardo: the exterior, the entrance portico, and a covered stretch flanked by the shops of the unique shopping center.

The dome of the Hurvà Synagogue.

RAMBAN AND HURVÀ SYNAGOGUES

These two synagogues are located right near the open portion of the Cardo, next to the minaret of the Sidi Omar Mosque. **Ramban** is another acronym of the name of Rabbi Moshe Ben Nahman, a great Talmudic scholar who arrived from Spain around 1267. The synagogue is the oldest in Jerusalem along with the Karaite Synagogue. It was closed by the Turkish government during the 16th century, then destroyed in 1948, and partially rebuilt in 1967 when it once again became a house of worship.

The **Hurvà Synagogue** (the word means "ruin") is located right behind the Ramban. Built in the 18th century by Polish Jews, followers of the famous Rabbi Yehuda ha-Hassid, it was destroyed several times, most recently in 1948 when the Arab League razed it to the ground. The synagogue we see today has been rebuilt in a recreation of 20th-century style it possessed before it was last destroyed.

TIFERET ISRAEL SYNAGOGUE AND FOUR SEFARDIC SYNAGOGUES

Just a short distance from the Hurvà square are the remains of the **Tiferet Israel Synagogue** (that is, "glory of Israel"). Before it was destroyed in 1948, its outlines were clearly visible above the city's roofs. All that remains today are three, richly carved portals. Nearby, are also the ruins of the 9th century **Karaite Synagogue**; the Karaites broke away from traditional Judaism in the 8th

century CE. The heart of the Jewish quarter is located south of Hurvà square. It comprises the **Four Sefardic Synagogues**, a center of worship for the Jews who arrived here after being expelled from Spain in 1492. East of the Jewish Quarter is the large square that reaches to the foot of the Wailing Wall.

The remains of the Tiferet Israel Synagogue.

The Western (Wailing) Wall at dusk.

Facing page: top, the Bar Mitzvah ceremony, which celebrates the coming-of-age of Jewish boys; bottom, Jews praying at the Western (Wailing) Wall.

WESTERN (WAILING) WALL

Symbol of Jewish faith and the object of Jewish pilgrimage from all over the world, the Western Wall (**ha-Kotel ha-Ma'aravi**) is a remnant of the western retaining wall of Herod's Temple Mount. It acquired the name "Wailing Wall" because during the long exile of the Jewish people from the city, they could return only once a year to mourn the destruction of the Temple. Throughout nearly two thousand years of exile, Jews from all parts of the world turned their faces in prayer toward this Wall in the hope of return. The Wall became the symbol of re-

conquest of the city and reunification of the Jewish State when, in June of 1967, the first Israeli soldiers reached it. It was an unforgettably emotional event in the history of the Jewish people.

Today, there is always someone praying at the Western Wall, whether throngs of people gathered for the holidays or just a few lingerers in the middle of the night.

One well-known custom associated with the Wall is to insert small papers, on which are written prayers, into the fissures between the monumental Herodian stones.

WESTERN WALL TUNNEL

At the end of the Six Day War, in 1967, the Ministry of Religious Affairs gave the go-ahead to excavation of the Western Wall Tunnel, an underground gallery showing the entire length of the Western Wall (about 500 meters). The work lasted many years and revealed hitherto-unknown facts about the history and geography of the Temple Mount. The excavations even unearthed a stretch of *roadway* from the Second Temple period, an *aqueduct* from the Hasmonean period, and other finds.

WILSON ARCH

Located to the left of the Western (or Wailing) Wall, this arch was named for Charles Wilson who discovered it in 1865. Beneath this medieval structure lies the original Herodian arch which supported the bridge connecting Second Temple Jerusalem's Upper City with the Temple Mount. Ongoing excavations have revealed another seventeen courses of the beautifully dressed Herodian stone beneath the present floor level.

Left, Wilson Arch, and bottom, the synagogue under the arch. Bottom left, one view of the Western Wall Tunnel.

The excavations along the south wall of the Temple Mount.

ROBINSON'S ARCH

The remains of this arch are at the southwest corner. The arch supported a staircase leading to the Royal Portico of the outside Temple enclosures on the side where the El-Aqsa Mosque now stands. The four niches in the base of the structure have been identified as money changers' shops (offerings to the Temple had to be made in the local currency). The stone, protected by glass, engraved with a passage from Isaiah probably dates back to the period of the Emperor Julian the Apostate.

JERUSALEM ARCHAEOLOGICAL PARK AND DAVIDSON CENTER

At the foot of the south wall of the Temple Mount are a series of archaeological sites included in the **Jerusalem Archaeological Park**. Also in the area, the **Ophel Archaeological Garden** excavations.

The excavations in this garden have brought to light the large *double door*, which is walled over and partly covered by Crusader buildings. It was the gate leading out of the Temple Compound, while the entrance, the Triple Door, reached by stairs as well, was over to the right. Among the various finds there is the *ritual bath* (*mikvah*), recognizable by its double staircase, an "impure" side for going down into and a "pure" side for coming up after the ritual. Remains of *Byzantine* and *Omayyad buildings* have also been found: the Omayyad palaces stood next to the southern wall. An ancient *city gate*, from the era of the First Temple was discovered near the street (Derekh ha-Ophel) that flanks the Archeological Garden.

Again in the Jerusalem Archaeological Park, near the Dung Gate, stands the **Davidson Center**. This center documents the history of the Temple Mount with archaeological finds, videos, and computer presentations. The reconstruction of the Temple of Herod, as it appeared before it was destroyed, is especially interesting.

The facade of the El-Aqsa Mosque.
Bottom, the Islamic Museum with the series of column
capitals preceding the entrance.

TEMPLE ESPLANADE

At the peak of what has been identified as the biblical Mount Moriah stretches the huge artificial esplanade that preserves the memory of the Second Temple erected by Herod the Great and destroyed by Titus' legions.

This large area that extends over about 12 hectares is in an uneven rectangle, partially bounded by massive walls. It is a holy place for all three monotheistic religions. For Christians it recalls two important moments during the life of Christ; for Jews it is the place where Abraham brought his son Isaac to sacrifice, and mainly because it was the site of Solomon's Temple, and the Second Temple. At the same time it is a holy place for Muslims: their third place of pilgrimage after Mecca and Medina.

EL-AQSA MOSQUE

The name means "the farthest" because, according to the Muslim tradition, it is the farthest point to which Mohammed went. The building dates from 709-715 when the Caliph Walid I had it built over the foundations of Solomon's palace. The original building had 280 columns arranged in 14 rows, but it was completely destroyed by three earthquakes. It was enlarged by the Templars who came to Jerusalem in 1099. At the end of the 13th century, after the Mamluks drove out the Christians it became the El-Aqsa Mosque, 90 meters long and 60 meters wide. The mosque has a silver dome and a low facade; the portico has seven arches that repeat the interior arrangement of seven naves. The columns supporting the **interior** arches are made of Carrara marble donated by

Mussolini on the occasion of the restoration work done between 1938 and 1943, at the same time, King Farouk of Egypt donated the ceiling. King Abdullah of Jordan was assassinated in here on 20 July 1951, and his grandson, Hussein, escaped the same fate thanks to a heavy decoration he was wearing on his chest. The bullet marks are still visible on one of the columns. In 1969 a deranged visitor set a fire inside the mosque so that lengthy restorations and repairs had to be undertaken.

ISLAMIC MUSEUM

It is located at the southeastern corner of the esplanade. It displays items of various provenance including *votive offerings*, *lamps*, and *weapons*. There is also an interesting collection of *manuscripts* and a beautiful *Mamluk Koran*.

The Dome of the Rock with its splendid gilded dome.

Bottom, a view of the interior of the mosque showing the two rows of pillars and marble columns surrounding the sacred rock, which, in Islamic tradition, is the spot of Mohammed's ascension to heaven and in Judaic tradition the Foundation Stone, the location of the Holiest of Holies during the Temple period.

DOME OF THE ROCK

In 640 the Caliph Omar ibn al-Khattab built the first square-shaped mosque, but in 687 Abd al-Malik ibn Marwan, caliph of the Omayyad dynasty, replaced it with a building of incomparable beauty, the **Qubbat es-Sakhrah** or, the **Dome of the Rock** (which is often, and incorrectly, called the **Mosque of Omar**). In the 12th century it was transformed into a Christian church called Templum Domini, but it was returned to the Muslim faith by Saladin in 1187. It rises in the large, rectangular enclosure known as *Haram esh-Sharif* (The Noble Enclosure) on a platform reached by four impressive staircases that culminate in elegant, colonnaded porticoes known as *mawazim* that is, scales, because according to Islam, scales to weigh souls will be hung on the Day of Judgement. Thanks to its position it is visible to all, and from all sides. The building is an octagon and all its sides are finely decorated; the four sides that correspond to the compass points each have doors with porticoes. The splendid dome in the center of the octagon was entirely gilded by the Caliph Abd al-Malik. The **exterior** has two overlapping layers of decorations: below, a colored marble band, and above, blue faience tiles with arabesques that Suleiman the Magnificent had made at Kashan in Persia to replace the mosaics of the previous decorations. The marble band is also a replica of the original 16th century decoration. The pediment was embellished in 1876 with an inscription praising the glories of Allah; the work was done by the famous Turkish calligrapher, Mohammed Chafid.

Via Dolorosa

Although the custom of retracing Jesus' steps to Golgotha began in the early centuries of Christianity, it was in the 16th century that the term Via Dolorosa (or Way of the Cross) came into use to indicate the approximate route Jesus followed bearing the burden of the Cross from the Antonia Fortress to the Calvary. The Fortress, Herod's residence, and also described as the seat of the Praetorium where Jesus was brought before Pilate, was destroyed along with the Temple in 70 CE by the Emperor Titus. Only bits of the original floor and the entrance to one of the four corner towers remain.

The First Station (*Jesus is condemned to death*). The First Station is located in the courtyard of the *el-Omariyya Madrasah* (school of Islamic studies) founded in the 14th century over the site of the Antonia Fortress. Every Friday, which is the Muslim holy day, it is the starting point for the procession, led by Franciscan monks, that ends at the Holy Sepulchre.

The exterior of the Chapel of the Flagellation (Second Station).

The Second Station (*Jesus is made to bear his cross*). This event is commemorated on the outside wall of the Chapel of the Condemnation which, like the Chapel of the Flagellation, is located in the courtyard of the Franciscan *Monastery of the Flagellation* on the right hand side of the Via Dolorosa, opposite the el-Omariyya Madrasah. The window above the altar in the **Chapel of the Flagellation** portrays *Jesus' suffering*, while the mosaic on the dome depicts a large *crown of thorns*.

The **Chapel of the Condemnation**, still has some of the stones of the Lithostrotos, much of which can be seen in the nearby Sisters of Zion Convent. The stained glass on the dome shows *Angels carrying the instruments of Christ's passion*, *Pilate washing his hands*, and *Jesus taking the cross*.

Going along the Via Dolorosa we come to the **Ecce Homo Arch**. Actually, this is the central part of the triple arch that Hadrian built in 135 CE to mark the entrance to *Aelia Capitolina*, the Roman city built over the ruins of Jerusalem. The southern arch, towards the Temple area is partially preserved inside an Arab building, while the northern arch can be seen in the choir of the Church of the Sisters of Zion. Above the part spanning the street

Left, the Via Dolorosa. Bottom, the interior of the Chapel of the Flagellation.

The interior of the Chapel of the Condemnation.
Left, the Lithostrotos and, bottom, the Struthion Pool,
located underneath the Convent of the Sisters of Zion.

is an Arab home. The current name dates from the crusades and refers to Pilate's words, "Behold the man."
Both the **Convent of the Sisters of Zion** and the **Chapel of Ecce Homo** rise over the site of the Antonia Fortress. From the back of the chapel we can see the remains of the fortified entrance to one of the fortress towers. Inside the convent, a flight of steps leads down to the **Lithostrotos** which, in the Gospels, is described as being opposite the *Praetorium*. It was here that Jesus was tried and whipped. This is substantiated by the fact that in addition to the little channels that served to drain off rainwater and carry it to the cistern below, the floor is marked for some of the games Roman soldiers used to play. One of these can be identified by the letter "B", the "game of the King", or "Basileus", in Greek.

The Third Station (*Jesus falls the first time*). On the site where Jesus fell for the first time under the weight of the cross there now stands a chapel built by Polish cavalrymen. The chapel is the seat of the Armenian Catholic Patriarchate, whose **Church of Our Lady of the Passion** presages the next station. In earlier days, a Byzantine chapel and a Crusader church stood on this site.

The Third Station.

Another view of the Via Dolorosa.

The Fourth Station (*Jesus meets his mother*). This meeting is recalled by a small Armenian oratory. The Polish sculptor Zieliensky carved the bas-relief in the fine *lunette* over the door.

The Fifth Station (*Simon of Cyrene is made to bear the cross*). An inscription on the architrave of the door to a Franciscan chapel recalls the episode of Simon of Cyrene being made to carry the cross.
The story is confirmed in the Gospels of Matthew, Mark and Luke.

The Sixth Station (*Veronica wipes Jesus' face*). The place where Veronica wiped Jesus' face is marked on the door of the Melchite chapel. The image of his face remained on the cloth.

The Seventh Station (*Jesus falls the second time*). Inside the Franciscan chapel that commemorates Jesus' second fall, there is a column from the Cardo. The chapel stands at the intersection that leads into the Christian Quarter of Jerusalem.

The Eighth Station (*The women of Jerusalem weep over Jesus*). A small, time-blackened cross is carved into the wall of a Greek Orthodox monastery.
It is here that Jesus said "Daughters of Jerusalem, weep not for me, but weep for yourselves and for your children..." (Luke 23:28).

The Ninth Station (*Jesus falls the third time*). A column next to the entrance of the **Coptic Monastery of Saint Anthony** indicates the places where Jesus fell the third time; it is in a high position, behind the apse of the Church of the Holy Sepulchre.

The last five Stations are inside the Church of the Holy Sepulchre.

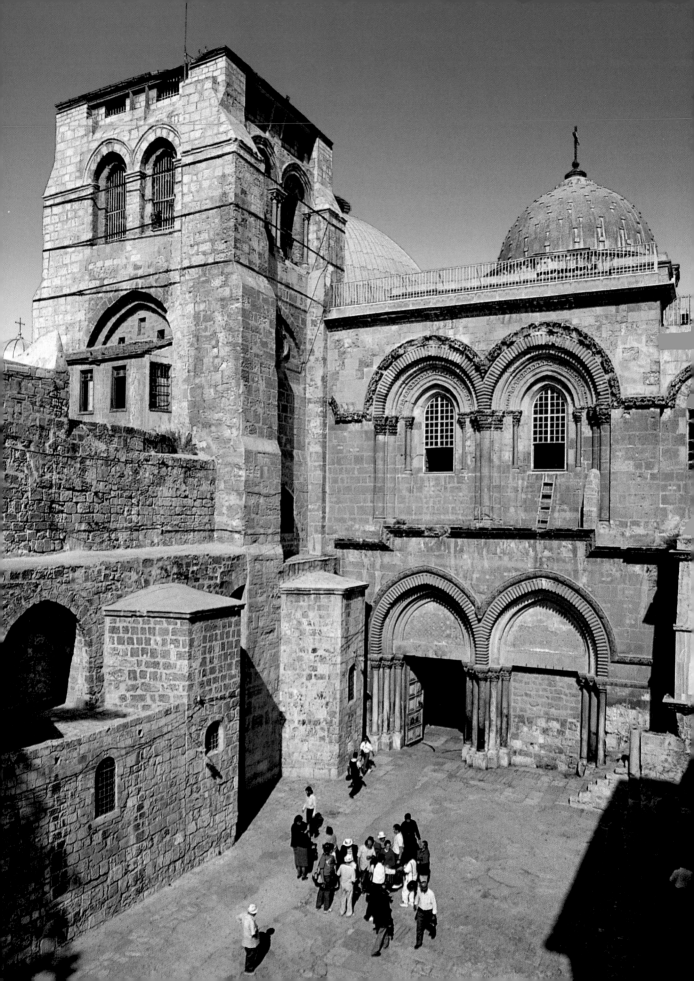

Holy Sepulchre

The Church of the Holy Sepulchre is the most sacred Christian place in Jerusalem. The quarry here was once an execution grounds outside the city's gates, with a hill plainly visible to everyone travelling to or from the city. It was called **Golgotha**, from the Hebrew word *golgolet*, (or Calvary from the Latin word *Calvaria*) or "skull", which is what the hill resembled. In addition, there is a legend that Adam was buried here. Near Golgotha were many stone tombs which had been hewn into the surrounding bedrock. The area was incorporated by the Emperor Hadrian into his new city, *Aelia Capitolina*, as a Forum and Temple area, dedicated to Jupiter, Juno and Venus. Hadrian built this new pagan city over the ruins of Jerusalem, which he had completely destroyed in retaliation for a major Jewish revolt. (It was also at this time that he changed the name of the country from Israel/Judea to Palestine.)

Fortunately, Hadrian didn't level the rocks into which the tombs were dug for the construction of his Capitoline Temple. Instead, he limited himself to filling those spares and leveling them off by placing large quantities of earth around them. By doing so, he created a base for the temple, an enormous terrace that preserved the tombs from destruction.

In 325 CE, the mother of Constantine the Great, Helena, and Bishop Macarius, travelled to the Holy Land to find Jesus' birthplace, tomb and other places important to Christianity. The excavations that the empress carried out here revealed the tomb of Jesus, His cross and those of the two thieves. Constantine had all the rocks and earth removed to expose Golgotha, where he placed a cross covered by a tabernacle, and the tomb, which he enclosed in a huge rotunda called the *Anastasis*, meaning Resurrection. The work was completed in 335 CE. The basilica which stood east of the rotunda was destroyed by the Persians in 614. Reconstruction began 15 years later under the abbot Modestus and the church remained intact until the Caliph Al-Hakim had it totally razed in 1009.

When the Crusaders entered the city on 15 July 1099, they found the church as it had been reconstructed by the Emperor Constantine Monomachus. As it did not seem suitable to them, they took on the task of rebuilding the church almost entirely. The new edifice was completed in 1149.

A ferocious fire devastated much of the church in 1808, but the western world, preoccupied with Napoleon in Europe, virtually ignored pleas for assistance in reconstructing it. The Greek Orthodox assumed control of the church and its repair, hence its present, predominantly eastern character.

Today, the inside of the Holy Sepulchre is divided among six communities: Roman Catholic, Greek Orthodox and Armenian (who together control most of the church), Copts and Syrian Orthodox. The Ethiopian monks have their cells and chapel on the roof of the church.

Left, the exterior of the Church of the Holy Sepulchre.
Bottom, the Stone of Unction.

The Calvary – The Calvary of today, accessible by steep steps, has two chapels side by side, one Roman Catholic and the other Greek Orthodox. On the Roman side, the **Chapel of the Crucifixion** commemorates the **Tenth Station** (*Jesus was stripped of his garments*) and the **Eleventh Station** (*Jesus was nailed to the cross*). On the Greek side, the **Chapel of the Calvary** commemorates the **Twelfth Station** (*Jesus died on the cross*). Under the altar can be seen the top of the rocky outcrop with a silver marker where it is believed the cross stood. In between the two is the *Stabat Mater* ("Sorrowful Mother"), in remembrance of Mary's agony at her son's death.

The Stone of Unction – Here tradition has it that Jesus was laid when he was taken down from the cross. His body was sprinkled with a mixture of myrrh and aloe and he was mourned by his mother before being laid in the tomb. This is the **Thirteenth Station** of the Cross (*Jesus is taken down from the cross*).

Christ's Tomb – Inside the aedicula of the Holy Sepulchre is the **Fourteenth Station** (*Jesus is placed in the sepulchre*) of the Way of the Cross. The aedicula is situated in the center of the *Anastasis*, and it is the result of centuries of changes made to an ancient Jewish tomb. The entrance leads into a larger room known as the **Church of the Archangel**. A fragment of rock marks the exact

Left, the Chapel of the Calvary. Right, the Chapel of the Crucifixion. Bottom, a view of the burial chamber and the aedicula of the Holy Sepulchre.

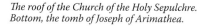

The roof of the Church of the Holy Sepulchre.
Bottom, the tomb of Joseph of Arimathea.

The Crypt of Saint Helena.
Bottom, the altar in the Greek Choir.

spot where the angel is supposed to have sat as he told the women about the Resurrection. The actual tomb chamber is small and awe-inspiring. It is here that Christ completed his earthly mission before his glorious Resurrection in accordance with the prophecies. A marble slab on the right covers the original rock of the tomb that was located in the garden of Joseph of Arimathea. Above the tomb are many silver lamps belonging to the Catholic, Greek, Armenian and Coptic congregations. Above the stone are icons depicting the Greek, Latin and Armenian versions of the Resurrection.

Coptic Chapel – At the rear of the aedicula of the Holy Sepulchre is the small Coptic Chapel. The Copts are Egyptian Christians (the name comes from the Arabic *Quft*, meaning Egypt) who follow the Monophysitic doctrine that was condemned by the Council of Chalcedon (451 CE). The Coptic Church recognizes only the divine and not the human nature of Christ.

Greek Choir or Katholicon – In front of the aedicula of the Holy Sepulchre is the Greek Choir, which stands on the site of the Katholicon, or Choir of the Canons of the Holy Sepulchre of the Crusader period. It takes up practically the entire central portion of the church and

is almost a separate place. A grandiose iconostasis at the top of a few steps divides it into two parts: one for services and one for the congregation.

According to ancient tradition, the *omphalos* (umbelicus or center) of the world is located beneath the dome of the transept.

Tomb of Joseph of Arimathea – This is the only part of the Holy Sepulchre belonging to the Ethiopian community. It is a small, rock-hewn tomb in the wall of the rotunda. Joseph of Arimathea, a wealthy member of the Sanhedrin, owned the tomb into which Jesus was laid, and was called "a good and just man who was waiting for the reign of God".

Holy Prison – This narrow space, known also as the **Prison of Christ**, is really an ancient jail annexed to the *Aelia Capitolina*. Tradition identifies it as the jail in which Jesus spent the night after his arrest in the Garden of Gethsemane.

Crypt of Saint Helena – This lower level chapel is dedicated to the mother of Constantine. It was built by the Crusaders and is supported by four 11th century columns. The chapel belongs to the Armenian Church.

KIDRON VALLEY

Just a glance at the Kidron Valley from the road that runs below the Temple Esplanade is sufficient for an understanding of how this place influenced the people of Jerusalem since its earliest days. The barren landscape, the unusual tombs carved into the rock or set amongst the olive trees give it an unreal atmosphere. Popular tradition maintains that the dead will be resurrected here on Judgement Day.

History, on the other hand, tells us that even if they are called the *Tombs of the Prophets*, these unusual burial places date from the Hasmonean period. Here is the **Tomb of Jehoshaphat**, of **Saint James** (actually this is the tomb of the *Bnei Hezir*, a family of priests; the name means "sons of Hezir") with the architrave resting on two columns, and the pyramid-shaped **Tomb of Zechariah**. **Absalom's Pillar** also called the "pharaohs' crown" because of its cone-shaped upper part, dates from the period of the Second Temple, and recalls David's rebellious son who "... in his lifetime had taken and reared up for himself a pillar, which is in the king's dale: for he said, I have no son to keep my name in remembrance and he called the pillar after his own name, and it is called unto this day, Absalom's place" (2 Samuel 18:18).

The Kidron Valley with the Tombs of Saint James and of Zechariah.

The centuries-old olive trees in the Garden of Gethsemane.

MOUNT OF OLIVES

The Mount of Olives rises beyond the Kidron Valley which separates it from the Temple hill. It is particularly important to Christians, since Jesus crossed its slopes many times as he went to Jericho and Bethany. The little Greek Orthodox **Church of Viri Galilei** commemorates the resurrected Jesus' descent on the Apostles.

GARDEN OF GETHSEMANE

It is one of Christianity's great holy places. The fact that even today there grow ancient, gnarled olive trees has stoked the belief that they may be the same trees that witnessed Jesus' last night before his arrest. In Hebrew Gethsemane (*Gat Shemanim*) means oil press, and evidently refers to the many olive trees growing there. The **Grotto of Gethsemane** which is supposed to be where Jesus, betrayed by Judas, was arrested, is just a short distance from the Church of the Tomb of the Virgin.

Notwithstanding restoration work done during the nineteen fifties, of all the holy places in Jerusalem, the Grotto of Gethsemane has best maintained its original appearance, that is, the way it looked in the days when Jesus walked the earth. From the 6th century on the place, which had been used as silo for a nearby estate, was used as a cenacle by some Christian congregations.

Inside the cave, with its interesting stone ceiling, there are three altars each of which has murals above it. Above the main altar is a portrayal of *Jesus praying with the Apostles*; the paintings above the lateral altars depict the *Assumption of the Virgin* and *Judas' kiss*.

The interior of the Grotto of Gethsemane.

The facade of the Church of All Nations.

The presbytery with the rock on which
Jesus is said to have prayed.

CHURCH OF ALL NATIONS

Jesus endured his agony in the Garden of Gethsemane before he was arrested. A sanctuary was built on the spot in the 4th century and later enlarged by the Crusaders. The present church, with its large, luminous *mosaic* in the tympanum, was built by the Italian Antonio Barluzzi between 1919 and 1924 on the remains of the previous structures. **Inside**, on the ceiling are the crests of nations who contributed to the church's construction. On the floor in front of the chalice-shaped altar is a *crown* of hammered steel thorns encircling a piece of rock where Jesus is believed to have knelt in prayer. The mosaic over the altar represents *Christ in agony*, those in the lateral apses portray *The kiss of Judas* and *Christ's arrest*.

CHURCH OF THE TOMB OF MARY

The church's spare lines go back to the age of the Crusaders (11th century) and is of Greek Orthodox denomination. Its **interior** houses the *Tombs of Anna and Joachim*, parents of Mary and that of her husband Joseph as well. The *rock-tomb of the Virgin* is found in a crypt, enriched with icons, precious lamps and paintings. The tombstone has three large holes in it permitting worshippers to touch the inside of Mary's tomb. It should not be forgotten however, that another tomb of the Virgin exists at Ephesus in Turkey: in fact, according to another version of the story, the apostle John took the mother of Jesus with him to Ephesus, where she remained until her death.

CHURCH OF DOMINUS FLEVIT

Here Jesus, nearing Jerusalem, stopped and wept over the destiny that awaited the city: "... and they won't leave you a stone standing because you haven't acknowledged the moment in which you have been visited" (Luke 19:44). The present church belongs to the Franciscans and was built by Barluzzi in the late 1930's over the ruins of a 5th century church. Remains of an ancient *necropolis* were discovered in the area, revealing numerous Hebrew, Aramaic and Greek epitaphs. Absolutely unforgettable is the view of Jerusalem from the window over the altar.

Top and center, the austere facade and the burial chamber of the Church of the Tomb of Mary. Left, the panorama of Jerusalem from the window above the altar of the Church of Dominus Flevit.

Facing page: bottom, the Aedicula of the Ascension with the encircling wall and the footprint rock preserved in the chapel.

CHURCH OF SAINT MARY MAGDALENE

Easily identifiable by its brilliant, onion-shaped gold domes, this White Russian Orthodox church was built between 1885 and 1888 by the Czar Alexander III in memory of his mother, Mary Alexandrovna. **Inside** are many beautiful *icons* and the *tomb* of the Grand Duchess Elizabeth Fyodorovna, canonized in the 1990s, who was assassinated in 1918.

AEDICULA OF THE ASCENSION

According to the Gospel, forty days after the Resurrection, Jesus appeared before his disciples and led them to the Mount of Olives and "... while he blessed them, he was parted from them, and carried up into heaven". This is where Jesus' life on earth ended; here the supernatural event is commemorated by a chapel which, since the 13th century belongs to the Muslims who consider Jesus one of the great prophets. The building has been markedly changed with respect to the original structure which had a double, circular portico and open arches. Inside the aedicula is the *rock* with a footprint said to have been left by Christ as he ascended to heaven.

Top and right, the gilded domes and the interior of the Church of Saint Mary Magdalene.

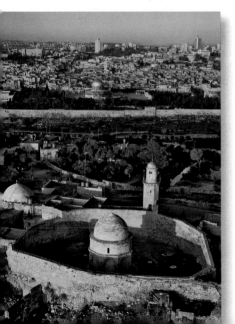

Ha-Ophel

CITY OF DAVID

Just outside the Dung Gate of the Old City is the village of Silwan (Shiloam). It covers the hillside (called in the Bible "Ophel") down to the Kidron Valley. This is where Jerusalem originated five thousand years ago. The wellmarked excavations of **Area G** show the visitor many levels of the ancient city, from the Canaanite, through the Israelite up to the Hasmonean period.

One follows the path down to the **Warren's Shaft**, where one actually enters the three-thousand year old Jebusite tunnel leading to a vertical shaft through which the ancient dwellers drew their water in times of siege. At the bottom of the hill, in the Kidron Valley itself, is the famous **Gihon Spring** where Solomon was crowned king.

Here is the entrance to **Hezekiah's Tunnel**, an incredible feat of engineering which channeled the waters of the Gihon through the rock under the City of David into the **Pool of Shiloah** where they were accessible to the city's inhabitants.

The Tunnel was built by King Hezekiah in 701 BCE. An ancient Hebrew inscription found here (and removed to Istanbul by the Turks) described the momentous project of digging the tunnel.

Top, the City of David and the south Temple wall in the model of Jerusalem.
Bottom, excavations in the City of David.

The Pool of Shiloah.

CHURCH OF SAINT PETER IN GALLICANTU

The name of this church recalls the episode in which Peter denied Jesus three times before the "cock crowed". This church was consecrated in 1931 and belongs to the Catholic Assumptionists, and was built over the remains of an older Byzantine basilica. It has been said, but never officially confirmed, that it stands over the house of the High Priest Caiaphas.

The church *crypt* has a series of grottoes, one of which has been called Jesus' prison. It is said that after having been questioned by Caiaphas he spent the night here, before being taken before Pontius Pilate.

The exterior of the Church of Saint Peter in Gallicantu.

MOUNT ZION

DORMITION ABBEY

This massive structure that rises on Mount Zion resembles a mighty fortress; it is topped by a high, domed bell-tower, a conical dome and corner towers. The church, built over the site where the Virgin is said to have fallen asleep for the last time, is the last in a series of buildings erected here over the centuries. It was completed by Kaiser Wilhelm II during the first decade of the 20th century based on plans by Heinrich Renard, based on the model of the Carolingian cathedral of Aix-la-Chapelle. The church belongs to the Benedictines. The highlights are the *mosaic* and the wood-and-ivory statue of the *Sleeping Virgin in the crypt*.

The Dormition Abbey.

DAVID'S TOMB

Since the 10th century it has been thought that King David, after his 40-year reign over Israel, was probably buried here, although it is more likely that he was buried on the Ophel with other Israelite kings. A church was built here in the 4th century and was later restored by the Crusaders. In 1524, the Muslims, who venerate El-Nabi Daoud as a great prophet, turned this site into a mosque and prohibited Jews and Christians from entering until 1948. The large *stone cenotaph*, covered by an ornate cloth featuring the Star of David, has several silver crowns, decorations for the Torah scrolls, symbolizing the kings of Judah who succeeded David.

CENACLE

On top of Mount Zion is the Cenacle, or Room of the Last Supper, where one of the most momentous events in the Christian faith occurred: the institution of the Eucharist. Also, seven weeks later, the Holy Spirit appeared here to Mary and the Apostles during the Pentecost. The Crusaders built the present room with its beautiful pointed arches, but in the 15th century, the Muslims took possession of Mount Zion, transforming the church into a mosque and prohibiting both Christians and Jews from entering for nearly five centuries.

Top, the crypt, with the statue of the sleeping Virgin, in the Dormition Abbey.

Center, King David's sarcophagus.

Bottom, the King David's Tomb building with its minaret and the Cenacle.

The Rockefeller Museum with its distinctive tower,
and one of the rooms in the interior.

ROCKEFELLER MUSEUM

Built with funds donated by John D. Rockefeller and designed by English architect Austin Harrison, this museum houses some of the most important *archaeological finds* in the country.

It is an elegant construction of pink and white limestone with an octagonal tower and a courtyard pool around which the exhibit rooms are located. It is located on the area where Godefroy de Bouillon pitched his camp before launching the final attack on Jerusalem.

The rooms contain archaeological finds dating from the Paleolithic period to the Crusades. Obviously, there is a wide variety of objects on display: from coins to pottery, from jewels to weapons, from sculptures to illuminated Korans, to Judaic antiquities. In the courtyard with the pool, there are several sarcophagi, and fragments of columns and capitals.

GARDEN TOMB

Often called "Gordon's Calvary" after the British officer who first saw the site from the top of Damascus Gate, this rocky outcrop and garden around it contain an ancient *tomb* which many Christians believe to have been the sepulchre of Jesus. From many angles, the hill resembles a skull, and there are various other features about the garden (e. g., large *cistern*, *wine press*, location near city gate) which make it a plausible alternate site to the Holy Sepulchre. Its serene atmosphere and lovely gardens are, for many, much more conducive to prayer and contemplation. Free guided tours are conducted on request. The Garden Tomb is administered by the Garden Tomb Association founded and based in England.

The Garden Tomb.

Russian Cathedral of Holy Trinity

Beautiful green domes topped by golden crosses characterize Jerusalem's Russian Orthodox Cathedral. An enormous stone *column* 12 yards long lays on the ground in front of it: probably broken off during construction work on the Temple of Herod. During the British Mandate of Israel, English authorities occupied part of the convent's apartments transforming them into offices.

The church stands on the site known as the Field of the Assyrians. It seems that Sennacherib's troops camped here in preparation for their siege of the city. Then, centuries later, Titus' armies camped in the same place when they destroyed the Temple.

Knesset

The Israeli National Assembly has its headquarters in this building which was inaugurated in 1966. Its construction was financed by James Rothschild and the artists Marc Chagall, Dani Karavan and David Palumbo contributed their works. The Knesset is composed of 120 members who are elected every four years. Facing the main entrance of the building is the large bronze **menorah** (seven-branched candelabrum), decorated with 29 scenes from the history of Israel. It is the work of the English sculptor Benno Elkian and was a gift of the British Parliament.

Supreme Court

Opened in 1992, this building is the seat of the Israeli Supreme Court. The strikingly modern design incorporates many elements of Middle Eastern architecture (domes, arches, and passageways) that create interesting plays of light and shadow.

Top, the Russian Cathedral and underneath the menorah in front of the Knesset building. The menorah is a symbol of light, in the Jewish religion, of the nation of Israel and of the mission of Jews to be "a light among nations." Bottom, the Supreme Court building.

The model of Jerusalem from the Second Temple period.

ISRAEL MUSEUM

This museum, designed by the Israeli architects, Alfred Mansfeld and Dora Gad was opened in 1965. Its modern pavilions fit in well with the green landscape dotted by olive and cypress trees. The museum is divided into many sections.

The **Samuel Bronfman Biblical and Archaeology Wing** houses finds from archaeological sites in the region, dating from the prehistoric period through the Islamic conquest. The **Judaica and Jewish Ethnography Wing** exhibits an outstanding collection of objects used in religious rites and of secular pieces.

The **Bezalel Art Wing**, dedicated to the fine arts, contain drawings, prints and paintings by foreign and Israeli artists dating from the 15th to the 20th century. This collection forms the link between past and present, with works by great artists including Cranach, Rembrandt, Monet, Cézanne, Matisse, Schiele, Chagall, Picasso, Rothko and Kiefer.

The **Ruth Youth Wing** is a very special place. It has its own exhibition gallery, and studios for the study of plastic arts; it also has a theatrical and multimedia workshop, that opens the doors to the future for its thousands of

Several statues in the Billy Rose Art Garden.

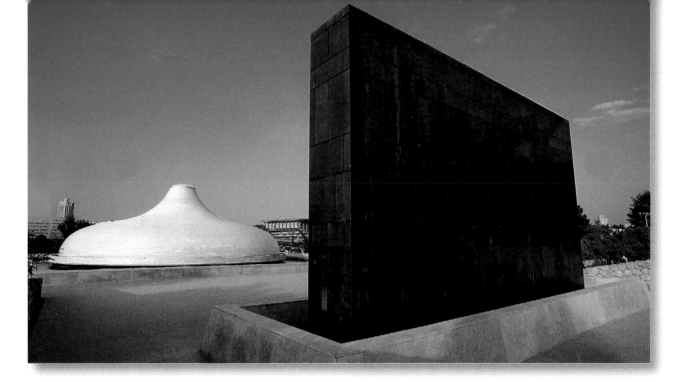

The exterior and interior of the Shrine of the Book.

young members. The **Billy Rose Art Garden** is dedicated to contemporary sculpture and contains pieces by Rodin, Maillol, Picasso, Moore, Marini, Wotruba, Vasarely and Turrel just to list the most famous names, as well as works by Israeli artists.

The museum also has exhibits objects recalling the diaspora of the Jewish communities, from various periods, and a gallery of artwork from Africa, the Americas, Oceania, and the Far East. A recent addition to the museum is a **model of the Jerusalem** of the Second Temple period that reconstructs the topography and architectural features of the city as it was before the revolt against Roman rule and the destruction of the Temple.

SHRINE OF THE BOOK

This section of the museum contains the famous **Dead Sea Scrolls**, two-thousand year old manuscripts that were discovered in terracotta jars in caves at Qumran.

The pavilion housing the scrolls was designed by the American team of Frederick Kiesler and Armand Bartos. It has a dome shaped like the covers of the jars found at Qumran, while the contrast between the white dome and the black basalt wall alludes to the dualistic concept of the cosmos divided between Light and Darkness, and the triumph of the "Sons of Light" over the "Sons of Darkness".

One of the most important scrolls found at Qumran is seven meters long: it contains the Book of Isaiah, and is the most ancient Jewish manuscript known today. Other scrolls deal with the rules of the Dead Sea Community, a sect that withdrew to the desert to live in strict observance of Mosaic Law.

Top and bottom, two images of the new wing of the Yad va-Shem complex.

The Hall of Names.

YAD VA-SHEM

This is a place of commemoration and homage to the six million Jewish victims of the Nazi regime. There are many components of Yad va-Shem (a *sinagogue*, the *Children's Memorial*, the *Avenue of the Righteous among the Nations*, the *Holocaust Art Museum* and the *Valley of the Communities*), including the **New Holocaust History Museum**.

Opened in 2005, the museum is housed in a triangular prism-shaped structure on an area of 4200 m². The exhibits illustrate the history of the Holocaust from the point of view of the Jewish people. At the end of the museum itinerary is the **Hall of Names** with the Pages of Testimony, forms for requesting information on Holocaust victims.

Outside there is a towering column, the **Pillar of Heroism**, dedicated to the memory of all those who resisted Nazism, with the word *Zkor* at the top, "Remember".

In the **Ohel Yizkor** (*Hall of Remembrance*), a low, reinforced concrete structure, the visitor will find the names of the main death camps written on the floor. An eternal flame burns next to a vault containing the ashes of some of those who died in the Holocaust.

Facing page: the New Holocaust History Museum and the Valley of the Communities.

A panoramic view of Ein Kerem. Bottom, the crypt inside the Sanctuary of Saint John in which it is believed the Baptist was born.

EIN KEREM

This small village, a western suburb of Jerusalem since 1961, is the biblical Ein Kerem, "Fountain of the Vineyard". Inhabited by Arabs, it was abandoned in 1948 and resettled by Jewish immigrants in the 1950s. This was the scene of the Visitation, when Mary went to see her cousin Elizabeth, who greeted the future mother of Jesus with the words, "Blessed art thou among women". Mary responded with the *Magnificat*, a song of praise to the Lord, inscribed in the **Church of the Visitation**, built in 1939 by Antonio Barluzzi. Ein Kerem is the birthplace of Saint John the Baptist. A fifth-century Franciscan monastery dedicated to him was built on the traditional site of the home of his parents, Elizabeth and Zachary. It was used as a stable by the Arabs but later restored.

SANCTUARY OF SAINT JOHN THE BAPTIST

The sanctuary, which is in the hands of the Franciscan order, dates from the end of the 19th century. The earlier Crusader building was destroyed by Saladin who turned it into a caravansary. The three-nave church houses some fine ornaments.

In the *crypt* is the **Grotto of Benedictus,** the presumed birthplace of John the Baptist. A marble star in front of the altar recalls the event with these words: "Hic precursor Domini natus est".

The exterior and interior of the Sanctuary of Saint John the Baptist.

HADASSAH HOSPITAL

In Ein Kerem is one of the most beautiful works of art of our day: the stained glass windows by Marc Chagall which were installed and dedicated in the hospital in 1961. The twelve panels, whose colors match those of the breastplate of the High Priest described in the Book of Exodus, represent Jacob's parting words to his twelve sons. These twelve sons were to become most of the twelve tribes of Israel (Joseph was not a tribe, but his two sons, Ephraim and Menashe, were to become half-tribes). With his assistant, Charles Marq, Chagall developed a special technique of using up to three colors in each panel, whereas before, each bit of stained glass had to be isolated by borders of lead.

Marc Chagall's splendid stained-glass windows at the Hadassah Hospital in Ein Kerem.

A view of Bethlehem.

AROUND JERUSALEM

BETHLEHEM

A few miles south of Jerusalem along a charming, biblical road, is the hilltop town of Bethlehem. The name Bethlehem has two meanings: in Hebrew, the House of Bread, and in Arabic, the House of Meat. On both sides of the road are vast, rocky pastures where shepherds tend their flocks of sheep and goats. One of these is aptly called the "Shepherds' Fields" because here the angels announced the birth of Jesus. It was also in these fields that the tender love story between Ruth and Boaz unfolded as narrated in the Book of Ruth. Their son, Obed, was to become the grandfather of King David, who was born in Bethlehem a thousand years before the birth of Jesus. For Christians, Bethlehem is a holy city because Jesus was born there. "In those days, an edict of Augustus came out for the census

The "gate of humility" that leads in to the Church of the Nativity.

of the entire empire." One of the principal functions of the Roman administration was to impose taxes. Therefore, the census ordered by Augustus, and supervised by the local governor Publius Sulpicius Quirinus, was certain to provide ready monies to the authorities. Since law decreed that every landowner had to declare his property for purposes of taxation, Joseph had to leave Nazareth and return to Bethlehem "... together with his bride, Mary, who was with child. While they were in that place, the moment of birth arrived and there she brought forth her firstborn son, wrapped him in swaddling clothes and laid him in a manger because there was no room for them at the inn". This is, how the Gospel of Luke describes the event destined to change the history of mankind.

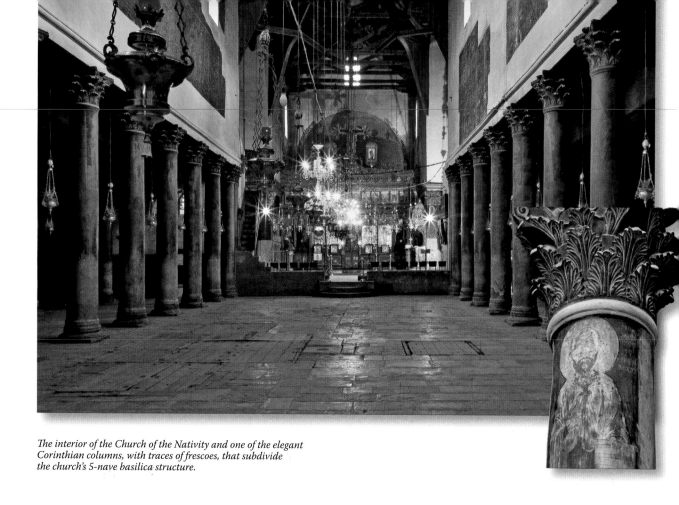

The interior of the Church of the Nativity and one of the elegant
Corinthian columns, with traces of frescoes, that subdivide
the church's 5-nave basilica structure.

CHURCH OF THE NATIVITY

The actual birthdate of Jesus is disputed: for Roman
Catholics it is December 24, for Greek Orthodox it is
January 6 and for the Armenians, January 18.
In contempt for the pilgrims who had venerated this
place since the earliest times, Emperor Hadrian, in 135
CE, consecrated the woods and caves here to Adonis
and introduced his own pagan cult. In 326, Constantine
the Great, after having the woods cut down, ordered the
construction of a basilica on the spot. The present structure is a combination of Constantine's basilica (much of
which was destroyed two centuries after its construction), Justin's sixth century renovations and later Crusader repairs. The basilica was miraculously spared during the Persian invasion of 614, because the invaders
found a painting of the three Magi, whom they took to
be Persians, decorating the pediment. In 1101, Baldwin I
was crowned Crusader king there, and twenty years later,
Baldwin II and his wife were, as well. Then came a long
decline. In 1646, the Turks melted down the lead from
its roof to make cannonballs. About the same time, the
Christian community decided to block up the main entrance except for a very small opening, to prevent the lo-
cals from riding into the church on horseback. The door

is only one and a half yards high, and is sometimes called
the "gate of humility" since one has to stoop to enter.
Inside the basilica, red limestone columns with Corinthian capitals line the double aisles on either side of the
central nave. Above them, one sees the remnants of *mosaics*, done in 1169, which have a gold background and
depict the ancestors of Jesus and the first seven ecumeni-
cal councils. Of these councils, only the first at Constan-
tinopole has survived in its entirety, while fragments of
the others, Nicaea, Ephesus and Chalcedon, can also be
seen.

GROTTO OF NATIVITY

This is the small grotto located directly under the main
altar of the church. In its small apse a silver star marks
the place of Jesus' birth.
Above the altar are fifteen lamps belonging to different
Christian communities. In a sunken chapel off to the side
of the grotto are two altars: the *altar of the crib* where the
newborn infant was laid, and the *altar of the Magi,* the
three kings who came to worship the newborn king.

The marble slab with the star marking
the spot believed to be the birthplace of Jesus.

The Chapel of Saint Helena adjacent
to the Church of the Nativity.

The Grotto of the Nativity.

CHURCH OF SAINT CATHERINE

Next door to the Church of the Nativity is the Roman Catholic Church of Saint Catherine. It was built by the Franciscans in 1881 over a cave where, tradition says, Saint Jerome lived when he was translating the scriptures from the Greek Septuagint to the Latin Vulgate in the 4th century. A *statue* of him can be seen in the **courtyard**, once part of a Crusader cloistered convent, outside. Saint Catherine's is where Christmas Midnight Mass is celebrated and relayed throughout the world via satellite.

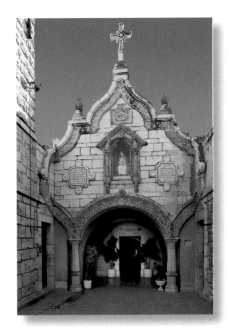

Facing page: the cloister of the Church of Saint Catherine and the faithful in the nave during Christmas Mass in the church.

On this page: the interior and the facade of the Milk Grotto Chapel.

MILK GROTTO

A Franciscan chapel is built around the grotto in which, according to legend, the Virgin took refuge to nurse the Infant Jesus. The dark stones supposedly turned white as a few drops of the Virgin's milk touched them. The grotto is a place of pilgrimage for Christian and Muslim mothers.

The Mar Saba monastery perched on the Kidron Valley wall.

MAR SABA

Mar Saba is generally considered one of the world's oldest active monasteries. On the walls of the Kidron Valley, about 12 km from Bethlehem, Mar Saba was founded by Saint Sabbas the Sanctified in 483 CE. Over the course of its history it has been destroyed and rebuilt numerous times; the fortifications date from the 19th century. The relics of Saint Sabbas are preserved in the *Church of the Theotokos*; the *Chapel of Saint Nicholas*, instead, stands on the spot where the saint founded the first church. Women are allowed to access only the Women's Tower of this Greek Orthodox monastery.

HERODION

Herodion was founded between 23 and 15 BCE on a plateau not far from Bethlehem by Herod the Great, who ordered construction of a fortress and a sumptuous palace. The archaeological site has yielded up a double *circle of walls* around the ruins of the **palace**, which commands a marvelous view of the surrounding area. The digs have also revealed traces of *baths*, other buildings used as storehouses and homes, a *synagogue* (one of Israel's oldest), cisterns, and a **second palace** in the lower city. But the most interesting discovery of all was made in 2007: the remains of **Herod's Tomb**, several fragments of the king's sarcophagus, and two other royal family tombs. The mausoleum was built over a pre-existing **theater**, of which the box for the authorities, complete with traces of Augustan-period frescoes, has been brought to light.

The upper city of Herodion from the large rectangular pool in the lower city's Roman garden.

A view of the lower city.

Hebron

The ancient name of Hebron is *Kiryat Arba*, which means "City of the Four" (from the area's four neighboring confederated clans). History has left a deep impression on Hebron: it was considered the land of Adam; it was the first territorial possession of the nomad Abraham, who is buried here with his wife and descendants; and it was the capital of the Kingdom of David for seven years.

Hebron is sacred to Moslems as well as Jews, both of whose religions consider their people to be the descendants of Abraham. In Arabic, Hebron is known as *Al Khalil* ("Friend of God"), signifying that God chose Abraham as his friend. Tension between the Moslem and Jewish communities erupted in bloody conflicts in Hebron between 1929 and 1936, in which many Jews were massacred. The British evacuated the Jews to Jerusalem, and the Jordanian administration subsequently prohibited them from returning to Hebron. After 1967, the Jewish settlement was revived. At present, both Moslem and Jewish worshippers gather at the **Haram el-Khalil,** the Moslem shrine which contains the *Tomb of the Patriarchs*. But tensions between the two peoples persist.

The exterior and interior of Haram el-Khalil, the Moslem shrine containing the Tomb of the Patriarchs.

The Dead Sea Region

DEAD SEA

Saline formations crop up from the water like ghostly coral; the rocky landscape is scorched by an implacable sun in a motionless, blinding sky. Nature reveals all of her calcified wrinkles and seems to be eternally punished by a damning torrent of fire sent by God. There is no life in the water, and all life on the land must adapt to this terrible blast furnace of salt.

The Dead Sea, the biblical Salt Sea, lies at the bottom of the Great Syrian-African Rift Valley, 413 meters below sea level. This relic of the Mediterranean, which covered the area over two million years ago, is the lowest point

Two views of the halite formations that typify the great salt lake landscape.

on the face of the earth. Its depth ranges from 380 meters in the north to 10 meters in the south. The atmospheric pressure in the area is the highest on earth, and there is 15% more oxygen in the air here than over the Mediterranean. Due to a very high rate of evaporation, the water of this lake has a salt content of over 30%, nearly ten times the salinity of normal sea water. Consequently, the water of the Dead Sea is extremely dense and swimmers find it very easy to float.

Besides salt, the water contains considerable quantities of other minerals that give it a bitter taste and oily consistency. When bathing in the Dead Sea, swimmers should be careful to not to allow the water to come into contact with the eyes. The Dead Sea water is renowned for its therapeutic properties and is particularly effective in the treatment of skin disorders. The dry, oxygen-rich air is also a valuable adjunct in treatment of respiratory disorders.

Mud bathing in the Dead Sea. The sea abounds in minerals with acclaimed therapeutic properties for treatment of skin ailments.

An architectural detail found in the inner courtyard of the sumptuous Hisham's Palace, a few kilometers from Jericho. Bottom, the baths at Alayiq, dating to the time of Herod the Great.

JERICHO

Ancient Jericho, which was first settled in the eighth millennium BCE, lies 250 meters below sea level and is situated at what is now known as **Tell es-Sultan.** Remains of defensive city walls and an impressive stone *tower* from this period can still be seen. Jericho is perhaps best known from the biblical narration (Joshua 6) of how Joshua caused the impregnable walls to fall by blowing shofars (ram's horn trumpets). According to the Book of Kings, the Prophet Elijah "healed" the unwholesome waters of the Ein Al-Sultan spring at Jericho with salt (II Kings 2:21). Modern Jericho is located nearly two kilometers to the south, on the site of the Byzantine town.

Three views of the digs at Hisham's Palace. The caliph's winter palace, the baths, the mosque, and an inner courtyard have been uncovered in the archaeological area. The baths contain a beautiful floor mosaic of a fruit-laden tree overshadowing three gazelles and an attacking lion.

QUMRAN

The remains of a **monastic settlement** inhabited by an ancient Hebrew sect, the Essenes, have come to light in an apocalyptically beautiful landscape on the northwest shore of the Dead Sea. The Essenes lived at Qumran in communal style from the second century BCE to 68 CE, the year in which Vespasian's 10th Legion occupied the area and scattered the members of the sect. Rooms used for various purposes have been identified: kitchens, storerooms, workshops, a refectory, and the scriptorium, in which the famous **Dead Sea Scrolls** were written. Some of the scrolls were found by chance in 1947 in a cave near the settlement ruins. They had been wrapped in linen and placed in carefully sealed jars, an indication that whoever hid them did all in his power to preserve them. This first discovery led to further exploration of surrounding caves, which yielded hundreds of manuscripts. These, however, were not as carefully protected; it is believed that the Essenes secreted them before having been unexpectedly forced to flee the site.

A panorama over the Qumran caves;
bottom, the archaeological area at Qumran.

THE ESSENES

The Essenes were an ancient Hebrew sect whose society was structured on a monastic model and whose the doctrines and rites were strikingly similar to those of the early Christian communities.

Essene doctrine prescribed a life of purity and asceticism far from the pomp and magnificence of Jerusalem. The followers of the "Teacher of Righteousness," as the founder of the sect was called, took refuge in the desert, where they lived in poverty and divided the fruits of their labors equally among themselves. They performed purifying rites such as baptism and frequent ablutions and studied the Holy Scriptures as they awaited the end of the world, which they believed to be imminent. Meals, which were taken communally, had a sacred character. The dining room was purified with water, a quite extraordinary practice considering the extreme aridity of the area. But the ancient inhabitants of Qumran were well organized from this point of view: a complex network of channels and cisterns, fed by an aqueduct from the western hills, provided water to all parts of the settlement.

The manuscripts, most written in Hebrew and some in Aramaic, are about one thousand years older than the oldest examples of the Hebrew Scriptures known until 1947. They contain all of the Old Testament texts except Esther, and also include the Deuterocanons, the Apocrypha, and writings in which the rules and doctrines of the Qumran community are described.

The remains of the fortified tower at the northwest corner of the monastery.

A cistern uncovered at the Qumran archaeological site. Various basins used for collecting water for ritual purposes have been found at the site.

The Shulamit waterfall at the Ein Gedi nature reserve.

EIN GEDI

Ein Gedi is an oasis abounding in fauna and luxuriant subtropical vegetation that has been rededicated as a protected area. The park area embraces a great number of springs; the main *En David* spring forms majestic waterfalls. Several grottos containing very ancient archaeological finds have been discovered nearby; also in the area are the ruins of an ancient synagogue and, at the kibbutz, a small museum.

MASADA

The mountain fortress of Masada looms over a desolate landscape at the edge of the Dead Sea. The name rings out as a warning and a promise in the phrase "Masada shall not fall again" pronounced by new Israeli soldiers at the swearing-in ceremony held annually at Masada. During the first Jewish revolt against Roman rule, a contingent of Jewish rebel forces ascended the mountain, took over Herod's fortress, and after the destruction of the Temple in Jerusalem in 70 CE withstood a three-year Roman siege. The end came only when the Roman commander, Flavius Silva, had an enormous access ramp constructed on the west side of the mountain, enabling his army to reach the fortifications. On the eve of the final Roman attack, one of the most moving tragedies in the history of mankind took place within the walls. For fear of Roman retaliation and dreading above all that their family members would be enslaved by the victors, the combatants of Masada chose suicide over being taken alive by the enemy. The premier historian of the time, Josephus Flavius, described their last moments: "While they caressed and embraced their wives and held their children aloft in their arms weeping and kissing them for the last time, at the same time, as if it were someone else who was acting, they effected their plan, consoling themselves with the thought of the tortures they would have

Two aerial views of the majestic ruins of Masada.

suffered had they fallen into the enemy hands. In the end there was not one who did not rise to the occasion and all killed their dear ones, one after the other... Then, unable to bear the anguish of what they had done and feeling they would offend the dead if they continued to live, they hastened to pile their belongings in a simple pile and set fire to it; then having chosen lots as to which of them would kill all the others, they lay down next to the bodies of their wives and children and embraced them as they bared their throats to those charged with killing them. After having killed all of them without wavering, the survivors once more drew lots and the one chosen by fate was to kill the other nine and finally himself... At the end the nine bared their throats to their companion who, when he was sole survivor, first looked around to see if in that slaughter there was anyone left who needed him; then when he was certain all were dead, he set fire to the palace, and gathering together whatever strength remained, plunged his sword into his body up to its hilt and fell down heavily next to his relatives" (Josephus Flavius, *History of the Jewish Wars*, VII, 8:6-8). Thus the last bulwark of the Jewish revolt fell. When the Romans managed to get through the smoking ruins they found nothing but 960 lifeless bodies awaiting them.

THE ARCHAEOLOGICAL AREA

A large archaeological expedition, led by Prof. Yigal Yadin, uncovered over 90% of the site between 1963 and 1965. Not only the ancient fortress, but also numerous buildings, palaces, storerooms and water facilities were excavated. Before the Great Jewish Revolt, Masada had been fortified by the Hasmoneans and subsequently converted into a luxurious stronghold and "impervious" refuge by King Herod. Today, we can admire the **northern palace** (Herod's magnificent private residence), the enormous **cisterns** excavated in the rock to ensure an ample water supply, the opulent **baths**, and the **western palace**.

The columbarium, where it is believed the non-Jewish soldiers of Herod's army were interred.

Several storerooms and the upper terrace of the northern palace.

The ruins of Masada, since 2001 a UNESCO World Heritage site, stand on a hill in a dominant position over the Dead Sea.

*A conduit that carried water
to the Israelite-era fortress at Tel Arad.*

TEL ARAD

This archaeological site encompasses
the most significant example of a Bronze
Age city in all of Israel. It is thought to be
the site of Arad, a stopping-place on the
Israelites' journey to the Promised Land.
The area was definitely of great importance in both the Canaanite and Israelite
eras, as is shown by the two nuclei of ruins that have been brought to light. The
lower city dates to the earlier period: the
buildings, streets, and city squares were
well-planned and enclosed within fortified walls. The *upper city*, instead, dates to
the Israelite period: of note here, besides
numerous inscriptions in Hebrew and Aramaic, are the vestiges of a **temple**, built
in the 10th century BCE and used through
the 7th century BCE, the tripartite plan of
which recalls Solomon's Temple in Jerusalem. Also of interest are a red-painted
stone tomb marker, about one meter in
height, found in the *Sancta Sanctorum*;
an altar in the exterior courtyard of the
building, and ceramic fragments bearing
inscribed names of priestly families.

A luxuriant oasis appearing seemingly from nowhere in the desert near Sodom.

Left, the formation known as "Lot's Wife," who according to the biblical story was transformed into a pillar of salt.

SODOM

Nothing remains of this ancient city. The only reminder of the Bible story of Sodom and Gomorrah is a *rock* that looks vaguely human: according to popular fantasy, this is Lot's unfortunate wife, transformed into a pillar of salt as she was fleeing with her husband and daughters from the rain of fire that God had sent down on Sodom (Genesis 19:26).

Today it is the site of the Dead Sea Works, which mines the area's deposits of potassium, magnesium, bromide, and other minerals.

Tel Aviv-Jaffa

Tel Aviv began in the early 20th century as a modest urban settlement on the dunes to the north of Jaffa. It grew so fast that it swallowed up the neighboring city and together they now comprise a single great metropolis: Tel Aviv-Jaffa. But back to history. In 1909, a group of Jewish immigrants to Jaffa purchased a stretch of barren land and began to build there, probably intending to create an urban complex more fitting to their needs since their lifestyle was Western and they had difficulty adapting to the Arab character of Jaffa. The new settlement was first called Ahuzat Beit but later became known as Tel Aviv (literally "Mound of Spring"), stressing rebirth and ties with the past. The name is mentioned in Ezekial 3:15 as the home of the exiles among whom he sat "overwhelmed for seven days." In many ways, the name was considered fitting for the first all Hebrew-speaking city in modern Israel. During the first half of the twentieth century, Tel Aviv's population swelled so rapidly that it became Israel's economic and cultural center and is now Israel's largest city. It was here that Israel's independence was proclaimed on 14 May 1948 at the house of Tel Aviv's first mayor, Meir Dizengoff. The house, which had been a museum since 1930, is now **Independence Hall**. Since the city was not planned in advance it is a stylistic hodgepodge, although there is a prevalence of functional style with garden city ideals and much of Modernism and the Bauhaus in the constructions postdating the 1930s.

Dominating the city is the **Shalom Tower**, from the top of which visitors can see all of Tel Aviv and its suburbs, including **Bat Yam** and **Ramat Gan** where sport facilities host Jewish athletes from all over the world every four years

The sunny beaches of Tel Aviv and a sunset over the sea.

Many of Tel Aviv's numerous hotels and other skyscrapers stand on the seafront boulevard, the fulcrum of city nightlife.

The major arteries and the wide boulevards of this modern city are constellated with kiosks selling fresh fruit and fruit cocktails and juices, the perfect pause for beating the summer's heat.

in the Maccabean Games. The cosmopolitan side and its cultural vocation of the Israeli metropolis emerges in its best light after the sun sets, when people crowd into the nightclubs and cafes, theaters and concert halls. The famous Dizengoff Street and its Dizengoff Center are the nucleus of Tel Aviv nightlife. Tel Aviv is the home of one of the world's greatest symphony orchestras, the Israel Philharmonic, as well as the famous Habimah Theater company. There are numerous cinemas, art galleries, repertory theaters, and historical buildings and other places of interest to visit, including the **Great Synagogue**, the **Carmel Market**, the Shalom Tower, and the museums, including the **Haganah Museum**, unique in its genre, the **Beit Hatfutsot** (Diaspora Museum), the **Tel Aviv Museum of Art**, and the **Eretz Israel Museum**. In 2003 the White City center of Tel Aviv was granted UNESCO World Heritage Site status.

Three images of the port of Tel Aviv with its wide boardwalk,
perfect for a pleasant stroll, admiring romantic sunsets,
or stopping for a bite at one of the many restaurants and cafés.

The skyscrapers of the Azrieli Center. The three towers are each different in section: round, triangular, and square.

DIASPORA MUSEUM

Opened in 1978, this museum traces the history of the diaspora of the Jewish community in models, dioramas, films, and multimedia exhibits, which do not attempt to document the histories of the single Jewish communities scattered around the world (about 3000 in all) but instead to provide an overview of Judaism. The permanent exhibition is divided into six sections devoted to the Jewish family, community, faith, and culture, Israel's relations with other nations, and immigration to Palestine prior to constitution of the State of Israel. Interesting *models* illustrate the synagogues of various Jewish communities in different parts of the world, and a metal *column*, hanging from the center of the ceiling of the museum space, recalls the persecutions suffered by the Jewish people over their history.

TEL AVIV MUSEUM OF ART

The Tel Aviv Museum of Art, founded in 1932, is now housed in the modern building designed by D. Eytan and Y. Yashar and built in 1971. The museum exhibits Israel's most substantial collection of modern and contemporary art. The Impressionist and Post-Impressionist section is particularly impressive, with works by Renoir (*Nude Seen from the Back*), Pissarro, Monet, and Van Gogh (*The Shepherdess*). Among the early 20th-century masters on display are Picasso, Klee, Kokoschka, and Pollock; also of great interest are the works by Marc Chagall (*Solitude*) and the collections 34 works by Alexander Archipenko. The "Old Masters" section, containing the works of 16th-18th c. Italian and 16th-17th c. Dutch and Flemish painters, boasts canvases by Canaletto, Rubens, Van Dyck, and many others. At the Tel Aviv Museum of Art you'll also find one of the world's most complete collections of works of Israeli art, from its beginnings to the pres-

Top, two of the exhibits at the Diaspora Museum: photographs of the great Jewish thinkers who enabled the growth of pluralism in the spiritual life of modern Israel, and the recreation of a Jewish wedding.

Left and bottom, two paintings in the Tel Aviv Museum of Art: Portrait of Madame de Vicq *by Peter Paul Rubens (1625)* and Ein Hod *by Yehezkel Streichman (1956).*

ent day, anywhere in the world, and sections devoted to architecture and design, photography, prints (including 150 works by Edvard Munch exhibited on a rotation basis) and drawings. The Tel Aviv Museum of Art comprises the **Helena Rubenstein Pavilion of Contemporary Art**, a prestigious venue for exhibits by contemporary Israeli and foreign artists.

ERETZ ISRAEL MUSEUM

The Eretz Israel Museum, founded in 1953, is made up of eleven pavilions, located around the Tel Qasile archaeological site, which exhibit materials illustrating various aspects of Israeli life and history. At the Eretz Israel Museum are a planetarium and pavilions devoted to the history of mining and metallurgy, ceramics, *numismatics* (with coins from 2600 BCE to the present), and the *Man and His Work Center*. The *Ethnography and Folklore Pavilion* exhibits items used in Jewish religious rituals and associated with traditions and ceremonies, many of which found at the Tel Qasile site. The *Glass Pavilion* displays glass produced in the Mediterranean area from the Bronze Age through the 18th century.

More paintings from the Tel Aviv Museum of Art's marvelous collection: right, The Shepherdess (after Millet) *by Vincent van Gogh (1889); bottom,* Fredericke Maria Beer *by Gustav Klimt (1916); bottom right,* Nude Seen from the Back *by Pierre-Auguste Renoir (1880-1881).*

A glimpse of the dig at Tel Qasile, where the remains of twelve cities, built one over the other, have been uncovered.

Two views of Rothschild Boulevard, one of the city's major tourist attractions.

TEL QASILE

Prof. Benjamin Mazar began the Tel Qasile digs in 1948; his work was interrupted in 1959 but resumed in 1971. The twelve layers exposed at Tel Qasile show that the site was continuously inhabited from the Neolithic era to the Early Arab period.

These mute witnesses of vanished civilizations include the remains of three *temples* and an *inscription* dating to 400 CE. The extraordinary vitality of this settlement, destroyed and repeatedly rebuilt, confirms the hypothesis that it was a trade center situated along the Phoenician caravan trade route; the cedars of Lebanon for the building of Solomon's Temple may have transited Tel Qasile.

In the 9th century BCE, the Egyptians this very ancient city to the ground and the kings of Israel rebuilt it. It was once more destroyed in 732 BCE by an Assyrian king, but rose again from its ashes to become, in turn, a center for the Hellenistic Greeks, the Romans, the Byzantines, the Arabs, and the Mamluks.

The artifacts found here show that the site's ancient inhabitants worked in agriculture, weaving, leather, and pottery. Various kinds of ceramic wares have been unearthed as well as weapons, writing utensils, and a statuette of the goddess Astarte. Oddly, no written documents have been found.

NEVE TZEDEK

Neve Tzedek is a quarter of southwest Tel Aviv that was founded by a group of Jews outside of the walls of Jaffa in 1887 (and therefore 22 years before the founding of Tel Aviv). Following a period of decline, the area was reclaimed and restructured and is now a pleasant milieu for a stroll along the characteristic narrow streets or a cup of coffee, a snack, or a meal at one of the many cafés and eating places.

ROKACH HOUSE

Neve Tzedek is the site of the House of Shimon Rokach, the enterprising founder of the district. It is now a museum, exhibiting period furniture, clothing, and photographs as well the sculptures of Lea Majaro Mintz, Rokach's granddaughter who was responsible for restoring the building.

JAFFA

Since 1950 an integral part of Tel Aviv, Jaffa is situated in the region Joshua gave to the tribe of Dan and is one of the oldest cities in the world. The name may originate in the Hebrew *yafah* or *yofi* ("beautiful"); according to one tradition, the city was named for Japhet, one of Noah's three sons. It served as a port for Jerusalem and it was from there that the prophet Jonah embarked for Tarshish. Jaffa is indicated in the Bible as the port-of-entry for the famous cedars of Lebanon used for building both Solomon's Temple and the Second Temple. It was at Jaffa that the apostle Peter resuscitated Tabitha at the home of Simon the Tanner. Greek mythology names Jaffa as the site of the rock to which the beautiful Andromeda was bound as a sacrifice to the sea monster before she was delivered from a terrible fate by Perseus. Andromeda may have been saved, but historical events have often left death and destruction in their wake. The port was occupied by the Egyptians about 3400 years ago, and later was a coveted objective for all the armies that passed through Israel. Destroyed by Napoleon in 1799, Jaffa was rebuilt at the beginning of the 19th century. It was governed by the Ottomans until the time of the British Mandate and was not returned to Israel until 1948. A favorite with young Israeli artists, modern Jaffa has a wealth of stores, bars and restaurants, exhibition venues, and places to see, including the **Great Mosque**, the **Clock Tower**, the **archaeological museum**, the **flea market**, the **artists' quarter**, and the **fishing port**.

Clock Tower Square in Jaffa's Old City.

The port of Jaffa.

The Mediterranean Coast

ASHKELON

A green oasis with splendid gardens and equipped with the most up-to-date tourist facilities, modern Ashkelon is a pleasant town overlooking the Mediterranean, a favorite for lovers of seaside resorts. Once upon a time, however, it was a Philistine port and the scene of interminable battles between the Philistines and Israelites. It was at Ashkelon that Samson lost his legendary strength when Delilah cut his hair. Ashkelon may also have been the birthplace of Herod the Great, who adorned the city with magnificent *colonnades*. Vestiges of these and other archaeological finds are preserved in the **Ashkelon National Park**. Ashkelon's port was of such strategic importance

The golden beach of Ashkelon, one of Israel's most beautiful seaside resorts.

that rival armies vied to conquer it at all costs: the city was repeatedly invaded, clashed over, destroyed, and rebuilt. The Mamluks destroyed the port for the last and final time in 1279: it simply disappeared, swallowed up by the luxuriant Mediterranean forest. The first archaeological excavations were begun in 1920. Today, Ashkelon has two distinct residential areas: the old city to the east known as **Migdal**, first inhabited by Arabs in the 19th century, and **Afridar**, a growing Israeli suburb on the coast.

A relief depicting Atlas and the goddess Nike, and several fragments of architectural elements found inside the bouleuterion *in the Ashkelon National Park.*

Several stone fragments and the Roman theater of Caesarea, today a renowned concert venue.

Left, a street in the Crusader Citadel: the ogival arches suggest that it was once a covered passageway.

The Church of Saint John at Bet Guvrin.

CAESAREA

The very name of this city evokes visions of the dawn of the Christian era, when Herod the Great dedicated it to Caesar Augustus and adorned it with fine marble and splendid monuments, the remains of which can still be seen. Caesarea was always considered a strategic coastal outpost and port by the many peoples who governed and controlled it over its history: from the Phoenicians, who established a base in the 4th century BCE, to the Crusaders, who fortified it after they landed here in 1101. The remains of the walls and **Citadel** built by Louis IX of France testify to the passage of Christian warriors in search of the Holy Grail, the precious chalice with which, according to tradition, Christ instituted the sacrament of the Eucharist during the Last Supper.

But the city's past is as full of tears and horror as it is rich in glory and memories. History became tragedy in the magnificent arena of Caesarea when thousands of Jews were thrown to famished wild beasts following the first revolt against the Romans and the Bar Kokhba revolt (66 and 131 CE), in which Caesarea was a center of resistance.

BET GUVRIN

Today's Bet Guvrin kibbutz rises on a site of some importance in the Greek and Roman eras. During the period of the Crusades, the site was fortified and the *Church of Saint John* was built; its remains are still visible, as are those of the crusader castle raised by Fulk IV, Count of Anjou. Not far from Bet Guvrin is the archaeological site of the biblical city of **Maresha**, where ruins from the Hellenistic period have been brought to light. The area is also pocked with myriad *caves*, hewn for many purposes including quarrying, and later used as burial sites.

A panoramic view of Haifa.

Top left, the splendid garden leading to the Shrine of the Báb at the Bahá'í World Center; right, the nave of the Carmelite Stella Maris Monastery church.

Bottom, the interior of the Cave of Elijah.

HAIFA

Haifa is located on the slopes of Mount Carmel overlooking the Mediterranean Sea. The city consists of three levels: the highly industrialized shoreline, the Hadar neighborhood, from behind the port area halfway up the mountain, and the lovely Carmel residential areas on the upper slopes. From here, the eye sweeps over the splendid panorama of the bay as far as Akko and, on clear days, up to the hills of the Lebanese frontier. Beautiful as it is, the Bay of Haifa also holds painful memories. During the British Mandate (1917-1948), the 1939 White Paper severely limited Jewish immigration into the country; thousands of Jews who were fleeing the Nazis were turned back from the port of Haifa and sent either to detention camps on Cypress or back to Europe; not a few would-be immigrants died at sea.

Haifa has dedicated an interesting *museum* to the victims and to those who managed to break through the British blockade.

Other tourist attractions include the **Cave of Elijah,** also called the Cave of the Madonna, since Christian tradition holds that the Holy Family sheltered here when return-ing from Egypt. Haifa is also central to the Bahá'í Faith, a monotheistic religion founded in Persia (Iran) in the early 19th century. Followers accept teachings from many different faiths and refute religious rituals and the clergy. The Bahá'i World Center with its gold-domed **Shrine of the Báb** and its exquisite gardens is one of Haifa's most famous landmarks. The Bat Galim quarter is home to the Carmelite **Stella Maris Monastery**. The current monastery church was built in the 19th century on a Greek cross plan; the interior is decorated with marbles and early 20th-century frescoes. Haifa also boasts many museums, including the **National Maritime Museum** exhibits illustrate the history of seafaring in the Mediterranean, the Red Sea, and the Indian Ocean; the **Haifa Museum of Art**, which since 1977 unites the collections of three previously-separate museums in the ancient art, modern art, and music and ethnography sections; the **Reuben and Edith Hecht Museum**, documenting the history of the Israeli people and more. Haifa is also the home of the well-known *Technion Institute* research center for science and technology.

Around Haifa

BET SHE'ARIM

The Bet She'arim archaeological site, discovered in 1936, comprises the remains of a city set at the summit of a hill and a subterranean necropolis at its foot that was used by the Judeans until the 2nd century CE. The ruins of a grandiose **synagogue** (2nd-3rd century CE), similar to the one at Capernaum, have been uncovered on the hill; the **necropolis** in the Cave of the Coffins contains 31 *catacombs*, each with a great number of tombs, that are accessed from the portal in the monumental, three-arched facade. Floor mosaics, paintings, inscriptions, and upwards of 400 sarcophagi, some of which are richly decorated (including the splendid "Shell Sarcophagus," so called after the elaborate motifs on the cover and the sides) have been found in the catacomb tunnels. The site also hosts a small *museum* exhibiting many finds from the archaeological area.

MOUNT CARMEL

The Mount Carmel coastal mountain chain, 39 km in length, embraces the Mount Carmel National Park with many nature preserves where visitors can enjoy uncontaminated nature and where animals roam free. Some very interesting finds referred to a prehistoric people (the Natufian culture) have been uncovered near En Hod, including many common burial sites containing about 90 skeletons.

One of the catacombs ("Cave of the Ascents") excavated in the rock of the Bet Sheíarim necropolis. A number of the catacombs are closed off by stones sculpted to imitate wooden doors.

Several deer at one of the many protected areas in the Mount Carmel mountain chain.

THE DRUZE

Although the sect is of Moslem origin, Druze doctrine incorporates elements of Judaism, Hinduism, and Christianity. According to the Druze, the divine principle may be manifested in human form, the last case being Caliph Al-Hakim (11th century); they also believe in the reincarnation of the soul. The majority of the Druze population lives in Syria and Lebanon; Israel counts two Druze communities in Galilee, in the Mount Carmel area and the Golan. The Druze consider themselves a distinct ethnic group; the Israeli government has officially recognized the community as a separate religious entity and the Druze are defined as a distinct ethnic group in the Israeli Ministry of Interior's census registration.

The port of Akko.

Top, the Khan el-Umdan caravansary.
Bottom left, several shops in the Turkish bazaar; right, the
ruins of the tower of the Montfort Crusader castle.

AKKO (ACRE)

The history of Akko, like that of most of the cities in the fertile crescent, goes far back in time. The first written evidence testifying to its existence dates to almost 4000 years ago: a variant of the name appears in the Tel el-Amarna tablets, which have been dated to the 14th century BCE ca. Throughout its long history, many conquering peoples have laid claim to this hospitable port: it thus became, for example, the *Ake* of the Greeks, the *Ptolemais* of Ptolemy Philadelphus, the *Colonia Claudia Felix* of Emperor Claudius, the *Saint-Jean d'Acre* of the Crusaders, and the *Akka* of the Arabs. In 1948, with the end of the British Mandate and occupation by the Hagannah (the Jewish self-defense organization at the time of the Mandate), the city once more took its ancient biblical name of *Akko* (Judges 1:31). Occupied by the Egyptians in the 15th century BCE, Akko was not conquered by Judah until a later date and is one of the places from which the Israelites did not drive out the Canaanites (Judges 1:31). During the reign of Ptolemy Philadelphus, Akko became a very active trading and fishing port, as well as an important glass manufacturing center; in fact, its glass manufactories became so famous that the historian Pliny maintained the material had been invented here. The Romans who conquered Akko in 48 BCE made it a major stopover on the *Via Maris*, the first paved road

they built through Israel, following the old route of the one of the major arteries of antiquity, which had been made unusable by Alexander's armies. From 636 to 1104, the city was in Arab hands. Taken by the Genovese fleet during the First Crusade, it was retaken by Saladin in 1187 and finally taken again by the legendary Richard the Lion-Hearted in 1191. After the fall of Jerusalem in 1192, Akko was renamed Saint-Jean d'Acre after the Knights of Saint John who, together with the Templars and the Teutonic Knights, were garrisoned there. It served as capital of the Crusader Kingdom of Jerusalem from 1192 to 1229 and was an outpost for many trading companies from Venice, Genoa, Amalfi, and Marseilles. This period of prosperity came to an end in 1291 when the Mamluks sacked and razed the city; Akko stood abandoned for about 450 years. A new period of prosperity came under the bloody ruler Ahmed Jezzar, the Bosnian adventurer who in the second half of the 18th century consolidated a vast kingdom extending from Tripoli to Damascus. His cruelty has become proverbial, but he was also an inspired town planner: he completely rebuilt Akko, not hesitating to plunder neighboring Roman-Byzantine palaces and ruins in his efforts to beautify the city; in fact, a great many of Akko's mosques, baths, and caravansaries are still embellished with capitals, friezes, or columns

MONTFORT

Near the border with Lebanon, on a rocky spur, are the majestic ruins of the Crusader Castle of Montfort. In 1228, the Montfort site was granted to the Order of the Teutonic Knights, who enlarged the castle and fortified it, but it was destroyed in 1271 by Arab Mamluk forces. Today, all that is left are the massive *tower* that protected the entrance, the remains of a spacious hall where the knights probably met, and the foundations of a chapel with a nave and two aisles.

from ancient buildings. To keep Napoleon's army at bay, Ahmed Jezzar had the city enclosed in a second circle of walls. During the 19th century, Akko figured prominently in the alliance between the Turkish empire and the British crown. Later on, the city declined, its port silted up, and the ancient capital of so many ephemeral kingdoms fell to the rank of prison fortress. In 1948, Hagannah forces took possession of the city, bringing it under Israeli administration. Signs of Akko's rich history are everywhere, from the **Mosque of al-Jazzar,** the largest in Akko, built over the vaulted rooms of the Crusader fortress and elaborately decorated with arabesques and marble, to the **Turkish baths,** now converted into a museum, and the once-sumptuous **caravansaries (khans),** reminders of the city's caravan trade. All these imposing structures attest to the commercial importance the city had achieved by the mid-19th century, when gem merchants from Venice, Marseilles, Amsterdam, Antwerp and London came here to buy their wares directly.

THE CRUSADER CITADEL

Undoubtedly, the visitor to Akko will be most impressed by the Crusader Citadel, the large fortress that was the administrative headquarters of the Crusader religious orders from 1191 to 1291. It is one of the most interesting and oldest examples of medieval Gothic architecture. In the times of Richard the Lion-Hearted and Louis IX, religious functions and councils of war took place in the vast hall, commonly called the **crypt,** which probably also served as a refectory for the Crusaders. Some of the brackets in the room are sculpted with the fleur-de-lis, perhaps the first usage of this motif in European heraldry. It would seem that the very Catholic Capetian kings of France borrowed it from Islamic heraldry; the iris was an extremely common Arab decorative motif and apparently the emblem of none other than the "ferocious" Saladin. Since 2001, the Crusader Citadel of Akko is a UNESCO World Heritage site.

A room in the Crusader Citadel.

Top and right, the exterior of the al-Jazzar Mosque and the prayer hall.

The Jezreel Valley and Lower Galilee

MEGIDDO

The *tel* of ancient Megiddo dominates one of the most important commercial and military trade routes of antiquity, the *Derech Hayam* of the Hebrew Scriptures, the "Way of the Philistines," called the *Via Maris* by the Romans. It linked the interior to the sea and was thus of utmost strategic importance. All of the peoples in the area fought to control it in all periods of history: Egyptians, Babylonians, Assyrians, Hittites, Canaanites, Hebrews, Persians, Greeks, Parthians, Romans, Byzantines, Arabs, Crusaders, Turks – all of them clashed on the Plain of Jezreel below Megiddo. Clear evidence of Megiddo's warlike past lies in its twenty strata of ruins, many of which were once military structures, and its fame as a place of battle echoes in the belief that it is the site at which the ultimate conflict between the forces of Good and Evil will take place: "And he gathered them together into a place called in the Hebrew tongue Armageddon" (Rev. 16:16). The word in fact comes from the Hebrew *har-megiddo* meaning "Mountain of Megiddo."

The tunnel built by order of Achab to link a well inside the fortress with a water source.

Bottom, the public granary with its double staircase.

An aerial view of the Megiddo archaeological site.

NAZARETH

In Arabic and in Hebrew, the name Nazareth means "guardian," perhaps referring to the town's strategic location above the Jezreel Valley (or Plain of Esdraelon). Later, through the work of the Franciscan fathers to nurture and preserve the spiritual heritage of the town, the allusion was extended to Nazareth's role as guardian of Christian tradition.

Although the area was settled as far back as the Middle Bronze Age, the town where the child Jesus lived was neither large or well-considered. Its inhabitants were called *notzrim* (the term, meaning "Nazarenes," "heretics," or simply "Christians" in modern usage, was a derogatory name used by one's enemies during the first century: Matt. 21:11), and is also often described negatively in the Gospels. Despite its unimportance, Nazareth was attacked by the Romans and later by its aggressive Arab neighbors. In 1099, with the arrival of the Crusaders, Nazareth became a bishopric and the administrative center of Galilee. It was repeatedly conquered and lost by the Christian warriors; the Christian buildings were destroyed by the Mamluks in 1263 and much of the town was abandoned. There followed a parenthesis of Franciscan presidium of the ruins of the basilica, but not until the order returned in the 17th century did Christians resettle the town.

The population of modern Nazareth is extremely varied. Moslem Arabs and Jews make up two-thirds of the town's inhabitants while the last third is comprised of Christian Arabs, Catholic Greeks of the Melchite rite, Greek Orthodox, Roman Catholic, and Maronite Christians, and other smaller groups, all of whom have their own places of worship.

Nazareth, with the dome of the Basilica of the Annunciation at the center.

The side of the Basilica of the Annunciation and the crypt containing the Grotto of the Annunciation.

The upper church of the Basilica of the Annunciation with the huge central mosaic of the Triumph of the Universal Church.

BASILICA OF THE ANNUNCIATION

The largest church in the city is the Basilica of the Annunciation, erected over the grotto where, according to tradition, the Archangel Gabriel announced to Mary that she would be the mother of Christ. The first church was built here in 356 CE by Helena, mother of Emperor Constantine, the first royal champion of Christianity. Other churches were built by the Byzantines, the Crusaders, and finally the Franciscans, whose sanctuary was pulled down in 1955 to make room for the fifth church constructed on the sacred site, the present Basilica completed in 1969. On the lower level of the church is the **Grotto of the Annunciation** where the words "Ave Maria" are carved on a column marking the place where the Archangel Gabriel is said to have appeared to the Virgin.

CHURCH OF SAINT JOSEPH AND SAINT GABRIEL'S CHURCH

The **Church of Saint Joseph** (or **Saint Joseph's Carpentry**) also belongs to the Franciscans and is built above older structures, one of which is traditionally identified as Joseph's carpentry shop. The honor is contested by the Convent of the Sisters of Nazareth and Saint Gabriel's Church, which both claim to be located on the site of the saint's workshop. This is not the only ecclesiastical dispute in Nazareth. According to Greek Orthodox tradition, the angel appeared to Mary near the **Well of the Virgin**, whose waters originate in the spring under the **Church of Saint Gabriel**.

FRANCISCAN MUSEUM

This museum exhibits significant finds uncovered during excavation of the Basilica of the Annunciation and the Church of Saint Joseph, such as ceramics, graffiti, and various architectural elements. Of special note, the five *capitals* crafted by different artists from Rheims for the Grotto of the Annunciation after the earthquake of 1170 but never used, and a *bust of Saint Peter* with a model of the church and the keys to the Kingdom (12th century).

The Church of Saint Gabriel; right, the Well of the Virgin.

OTHER RELIGIOUS SHRINES

Other religious buildings which merit a visit are the **Salesian Church**, considered a masterpiece of 20th-century architecture, the **Coptic Church**, the **Maronite Church**, the chapel known as **Mensa Christi**, and the **White Mosque**. The latter stands on the remains of the synagogue where a crowd of Jesus' fellow citizens attempted to cast Him over a cliff (Luke 4:14-31). The **Church of Our Lady of Fear** stands on the site where Mary is said to have stood watching in fear.

*The Jezreel Valley, with the ruins of Megiddo
in the foreground against the backdrop of Mount Tabor.*

MOUNT TABOR

The solitary crest of Mount Tabor looms over the Jezreel Valley in a region where every stone seems imbued with historical and religious significance. The name in Arabic, *Jebel Tor* ("mountain of the bull"), recalls an ancient Phoenician cult and hints at the mount's early, albeit pagan, sacred designation. The name of Tabor appears frequently in the Bible: the mountain marked the ancient boundar-

ies between the tribal territories of Zebulun, Issachar, and Naphtali (Joshua 19:10, 17, 32); on it the prophetess Deborah ordered Barak to call together ten thousand warriors and declare war against the army of Jabin, king of Canaan, who had oppressed the children of Israel for twenty years (Judges 4:1-16); and the prophet Hosea mentions it when he reproves the Israelite chiefs for their idolatrous corrup-

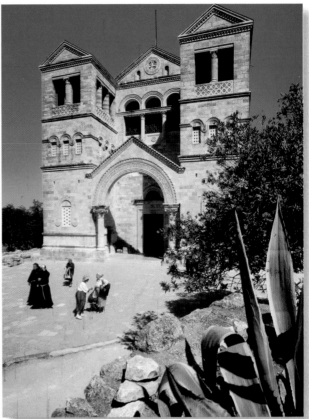

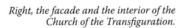

*Right, the facade and the interior of the
Church of the Transfiguration.*

tion (Hosea 5:1). Lastly, tradition has it that the miracle of the transfiguration of Christ took place on Mount Tabor (Matthew 17:1-5; Luke 9:28-35). In remembrance of this event, the **Church of the Transfiguration** was built here in 1923, the last in a series of buildings that were destroyed one by one over history, as so much architecture in the Israeli territory has been.

The Sea of Galilee
(Lake Tiberias)

The Sea of Galilee, and the city of Tiberias on its western shore, lie within the Great Syrian-African Rift Valley. The area's temperate climate, natural beauty, and abundance of therapeutic thermal springs have made the lake and its environs a favorite health and holiday resort. The waters of the lake have a maximum depth of 49 meters and provide most of the country's fresh water supply, as well as great fishing. There is normally a pleasant breeze during the hot season, but sudden violent storms sometimes brew out of nowhere late in the afternoons, as they apparently did also in Christ's time: "And behold, there arose a great tempest in the sea, insomuch that the ship was covered with the waves but he was asleep. And his disciples came to him and awoke him saying, Lord, save us we perish. And he saith unto them, Why are ye fearful, O

The Sea of Galilee, also known as Lake Tiberias.

The remains of the synagogue at the Korazim archaeological site.

KORAZIM

This archaeological area, on the basalt plain that dominates the Sea of Galilee, centers on the remains of the ancient town of Korazim, cited in the Bible in conjunction with Capernaum and Beersheba because its inhabitants were chastised by Jesus for their lack of faith. The site contains the ruins of a basalt **synagogue** on an nave-and-two-aisle plan, decorated with geometric and floral motifs and figures of animals. The foremost members of the ancient community sat on the basalt *Throne of Moses*. Excavations near the synagogue have uncovered a ritual bath, a cistern, and a storehouse.

ye of little faith? Then he arose, and rebuked the winds and the sea, and there was a great calm" (Matthew 8:23-26). Generally, however, the lakeshore provided a serene setting for Christ's teaching. The Gospels recount many episodes set here, including the meeting of James, John, and Simon, the miraculous catch of fish, the multiplication of the loaves and fishes, and walking on the water.

The South Gate of the ancient city of Tiberias.

TIBERIAS

In 18 CE, Herod Antipas founded the city of Tiberias, which was destined to become one of the most important centers of Jewish learning and culture after the destruction of the Temple. The Jerusalem Talmud was largely completed here in the 4th century and vowel symbols were added to the Hebrew alphabet. After having been destroyed more than once by massive earthquakes, the city was rebuilt further north, on the site of what is now called the Old City, while the remains of Roman Tiberias lie near **Hammat Tiberias**, the spa area located about 2 km from the city center. Hammat, an urban center much older than Tiberias, is also the site of the **excavations of the city of Herod Antipas** and an outstanding gem of Greek-Byzantine art, the **Great Synagogue (or Severus Synagogue)** embellished with precious floor *mosaics*.

Two details of the "zodiac mosaic" discovered in the Great Synagogue at Hammat Tiberias: top, the female bust representing one of the four seasons; bottom, the sign of Pisces.

CAPERNAUM

Capernaum, where Christ went to live after he left Nazareth, is located on the northern shore of the Sea of Galilee near the ancient *Via Maris* route to Syria. The Gospels contain many passages about Jesus' teaching and miracles in Capernaum, although he chastised the inhabitants for their lack of belief and repentance: "And thou, Capernaum, which art exalted until heaven, shalt be brought down to hell, for if the mighty works which have been done in thee had been done in Sodom, it would have remained until this day" (Matthew 11:23). Evidence of the town's splendor in historical times can be seen in the ancient **synagogue,** one of the earliest and best preserved of the Galilean temples. It is not, however, the one where Jesus first taught his disciples (Mark 1:21) nor the one built by the centurion whose servant was miraculously healed (Luke 7:5). It dates from the fourth century, probably to the time of Emperor Julian, when the Imperial government gave the Jewish community permission to reconstruct the original synagogue. The use of ornamental motifs such as eagles, lions, griffins, dates, acanthus, shells, etc., would seem to confirm the hypothesis that the synagogue benefited from Imperial funding.

A fragment of the frieze in the Capernaum synagogue representing a vase and bunches of grapes.

The nave and an aisle in the ancient synagogue.

KURSI

Kursi preserves the ruins of a large **monastery** dating to the 5th century and probably destroyed in the 7th. The monastery is Israel's largest (123 x 145 m) and was once decorated with mural paintings. The beautiful *mosaic* floor of the church, with its geometric decoration, still thrills visitors. Christian tradition tells us that Kursi was the site where Jesus drove evil spirits out of a man possessed and sent them into a herd of pigs, which then drowned in the waters of the Sea of Galilee.

Several structures of the Byzantine monastery at Kursi.

The Church of the Beatitudes on the Mount of the same name.

MOUNT OF THE BEATITUDES

On this mountain, not far from Tabgha, stands the **Church of the Beatitudes**, the name of which recalls the Sermon on the Mount during which Jesus intoned the Lord's Prayer as reported in the Gospel according to Matthew. The current church, on an octagonal plan, was designed by A. Barluzzi and built in 1938. The ambulatory is in black basalt, the columns of the portico are in travertine, and the arches in white Nazareth stone. In the interior, each side is dedicated to one of the eight Beatitudes with which the sermon begins. From its position on high, the church grounds offer a marvelous panorama of the entire surrounding area.

TABGHA

The name is an Arabic mispronunciation of the original Greek *Heptapegon* ("seven springs"). Five springs are still discernible but they are salty, which may explain why the area never attracted large-scale settlement. One tradition has it that Job was healed of his ills in these therapeutic springs. But Tabgha is more famous in Christian tradition as the site of the multiplication of the loaves and fishes. In memory of this extraordinary event, a small chapel was built here in the 4th century but was replaced by a large monastery and church in the 5th. The complex has been excavated and restored; parts of the original, resplendent *mosaic floors*, in which animals and plants are represented with an incredibly refined sense of color and workmanship, are enclosed in the new **Church of the Multiplication**. The Benedictine order's monastery in Tabgha is flanked by the Franciscan **Church of the Primacy of Saint Peter**, where Christ is said to have reappeared to his disciples for the third time after the Resurrection.

Three images of the Church of the Multiplication: the facade, the interior, and a detail of the mosaic floor decoration.

A group receiving baptism at Yardenit, the point at which the Jordan River flows out of the Sea of Galilee and where, according to tradition, Jesus was baptized by Saint John the Baptist.

A view of the Jordan Valley.

The exterior walls of the Belvoir Fortress, in a strategic position over the Jordan Valley.

The Jordan Valley

BELVOIR

The Belvoir Fortress is the only Crusader castle in Israel to have been completely excavated. It was built in 1168 by the Hospitalier knights, who exploited its dominant strategic location to defend the roads that crossed the Jordan Valley. The castle resisted two attacks by Saladin but finally fell into Muslim hands in 1189; the defenders who surrendered were permitted to retreat to Tyre. The fortress is encircled by a *double circle of walls*: the external five-sided fortification with mighty towers at the vertices and an internal wall in the form of a square. The castle was also equipped with a cistern and

The floor mosaic in the Bet Alfa synagogue.

underground tunnels connecting to the surrounding countryside, features which permitted it to resist prolonged sieges. Several sculptures from the Crusader era (mid-12th century) were discovered in the *church*, but are on exhibit at the Rockefeller Museum of Jerusalem and not at the site.

BET SHE'AN

The vestiges of ancient Bet She'an stand atop the *tel el-Husn* and at the foot of this "Mound of the Fortress." The city, which was located on an extremely important communications artery, was inhabited without pause for about 5000 years; an astounding 18 archaeological strata dating from 3500 BCE to the Arab era have been explored. The ruins on the *tel* include a Canaanite temple (1350 BCE ca.) with a dedication to the Canaanite god Mekal. The area at the foot of the tell was built up beginning in the 3rd century BCE; among the sights here are the **Roman theater**, one of Israel's largest and best-preserved with a 7000-spectator capacity; the Byzantine-era **baths**; the **Via Palladio**, an elegant street running through the center of the city; a *Roman temple*

A detail of the western inner courtyard of the Belvoir Fortress.

Bet Alfa

The Bet Alfa archaeological site holds the ruins of a Byzantine-era **synagogue** that was discovered in 1928 during construction work at the Hefzi-Bah kibbutz. The structure consists of a courtyard and a narthex that lead into the central rectangular building, which is divided into three aisles headed by a semicircular apse; it is probable that the entrance to the women's gallery was in the western aisle. A beautiful **floor mosaic** has been uncovered in the synagogue: an inscription in Aramaic close by the entrance dates it to the Justinianean era (6th century), while another inscription, in Greek, cites the names of the authors of the work as "Marianus and his son Hanina." The mosaic is divided into three panels framed in a cornice decorated with geometric motifs. The first panel represents the Ark of the Covenant and several ritual objects (for example, a menorah). The center panel depicts the twelve signs of the zodiac set around the chariot of the sun god Apollo; figures symbolizing the seasons are set in the corners. The last panel depicts the sacrifice of Isaac.

The remains of the baths and Via Palladio at Bet She'an.

perhaps consecrated to Dionysus; a *nymphaeum* (2nd century CE); a **Roman amphitheater** used for gladiator combats; and other buildings dating to the city's Byzantine period. An interesting **museum** in the archeological area exhibits finds from the digs, including fragments of mosaics (including the very beautiful *Leontis mosaic*). The Bet She'an site also stages interesting son-et-lumière shows for visitors.

A copy of the mosaic of Tyche, one of the Fates, found in the exedra at Bet She'an. Right, the Roman theater of Samaria.

SAMARIA-SEBASTE

The Samaria archaeological site, located close to today's Arab village of Sebastiya, is enclosed by the remains of the fortification raised when Samaria was the capital of the Kingdom of Israel (9th-8th c. BCE). The star feature inside the walls of ancient Samaria, renamed Sebaste by Herod, is the **acropolis**, where the *Temple of Augustus* or *Augusteum*, built by order of Herod in 25 BCE, once stood alongside other buildings and the *royal palace* of the King of Israel. The acropolis is served by a *Roman street* that was once flanked by more than 600 Corinthian columns. All that remains of the Roman **forum** is a portion of the colonnade on the western side and the **basilica** in which public meetings were held. Not far from the forum is the Roman **theater** and a **Hellenistic tower**, one of the most beautiful in Palestine; traces of a *stadium* have also been found. The Samaria site is also very highly considered because it is believed to be the burial place of Saint John the Baptist (in the *Church of Saint John*, built over the supposed tomb and transformed into a mosque after the Arab conquest).

The interior of the Ari Ashkenazi Synagogue of Safed.

Northern Galilee

SAFED

Safed, on the western slope of Mount Canaan, is the highest city in Israel and is known as the city of Jewish mysticism. When the Jews were expelled from Spain in 1492, Safed was under tolerant Moslem rule and offered refuge to

many individuals, including men of great talent and intellect. Among them were Isaac Luria, Haim Vital, Moshe Cordovero, Israel Najara, and Joseph Caro, who dedicated themselves to the study of the holy texts, particularly the Pentateuch. They studied and developed the Kaballah in an attempt to unlock the secret, mystical truths contained in the scriptures.

Today the city is divided into well-defined districts, including the **Citadel quarter** (Hametsuda), the **quarter of the old synagogues,** the **artists' quarter** and the **suburb of Canaan**, all of which offers picturesque walks through hilly mazes of narrow streets.

The Old City of Safed, with Mount Meron in the background.

The center portal and several columns of the synagogue at Bar'am.

BAR'AM

The **synagogue** at the Bar'am archaeological site, located close to the Lebanese border, is one of the oldest in Galilee. The basalt facade is intact up to the second story level. A portico stands in front of the facade, whose three portals, all with richly decorated framing cornices, open in the direction of Jerusalem. The interior is divided into a nave and two aisles. Near the synagogue are the remains of a *Maronite village* that was evacuated by the Israeli army in 1948 for security reasons, but the village **church** is still the spiritual center of the Maronite community.

A narrow street in the Old City of Safed.

TEL HAZOR

The Ayelet Hashahar kibbutz, founded in 1918 near the archaeological site of Tel Hazor, maintains a **museum** of fascinating artifacts gathered from the tell, which is all that remains of Hazor, the most powerful city in the Canaan at the time of Joshua's entry into the region. Vases, jewelry, spearheads, and basalt statuettes have been found during excavation of the site, which began in 1928. The digs have brought to light a *lower city* and an *acropolis*, connected by a tunnel running 38 meters down through the rock, many princely *tombs*, a *palace*, a great *temple* with numerous cult objects, and the *tomb of the King Jabin* of Hazor, named in the Book of Joshua (11:10) and the Book of Judges (4:2).

Tel Hai is renowned for the monument known as the "Lion of Judah," built to commemorate Joseph Trumpeldor, a Russian Jewish combatant killed in 1920 during an engagement with a group of Bedouins who had attacked the village.

A colonnaded building (perhaps a warehouse) from the Israelite period, at Tel Hazor.

The Golan Heights

MOUNT HERMON

Bordered on the west by the Sea of Galilee and the River Jordan, on the north by Mount Hermon, on the east and on the south by the Raqqad and Yarmuk Rivers, the Golan Heights mark the extreme northern boundary of the State of Israel. Always renowned for its fertility – the Golan area is the historical Bash'an of the Bible – it is now cultivated by over twenty Jewish settlements founded since the 1967 Six Day War when Israel conquered the area. Once the Syrian military withdrew from the Heights, the only previous settlers who remained are a few enclaves of Druze and Circassian farmers.

The Golan Heights are dominated by Mount Hermon (2224 m), which rises in Israeli territory. It is a favorite winter sport resort since its slopes are often snow-covered from November to March. The River Jordan and two of its main upstream tributaries spring from the slopes of Mount Hermon, fed by the melting winter snows. The river flows downward to the Sea of Galilee, 210 meters below sea level, and finally to the Dead Sea.

The snow-capped Mount Hermon.

A wind farm on the Golan Heights.

Facing page: fields in the Metulla area, near the Lebanon border, overshadowed by Mount Hermon.

The ruins of Nimrod's Castle.

Left, the falls at Banias.

BANIAS

Green with woods and loud with the gurgling song of streams and waterfalls, Banias is a natural sanctuary tucked into the lower slopes of Mount Hermon. The Canaanites who first lived here worshipped a water god; the Greeks who came later dedicated the area to the nature god Pan; the niches of the god's *temenos* near the main spring are still in clear evidence. "Banias" is apparently the Arabic mispronunciation of the ancient Greek name for the spring, *Paneas*. The nearby Roman city was known as *Caesarea Philippi*, and as such is mentioned in the Gospels (Matthew 16:13; Mark 8:27). After having been partially destroyed by an earthquake in the 13th century, Banias was refortified by the Arabs. It was eventually occupied by the Crusaders, who also took over the fortress on the nearby Subeiba ridge (**Nimrod's Castle**).

NIMROD'S CASTLE

According to local legend, the first mountain-top fortress was built the king of Babel, son of Cam, "the first to hold power above the earth," on a ridge in the Mount Hermon highlands; the ruins we see today date to the 13th century. When the Crusaders left, the fortress fell into the hands of the secret Hashshashin sect, whose members were addicted to hashish and were often involved in political murders. Their very name became a symbol of violence, the origin of the word "assassin." The imposing remains of the castle still stand as silent witnesses to its mysterious and fascinating past. Visitors can explore the keep, the inner fortress, and a secret passage, built of huge stone blocks, that led to the exterior of the castle.

The luxuriantly green Hula Valley.

THE HULA VALLEY

In 1956, Israel's first nature preserve was established here in the area around the swampy Lake Hula after reclamation work in the valley. The protected area shelters numerous species of fauna, in particular migratory birds (such as the storks and pelicans that stop here on their way from Europe to Africa and vice-versa), in the recreated papyrus swampland and "little Hula lake" with its water lilies and other wetland flora native to the area.

The Negev

BEERSHEBA

Capital of the arid region of the Negev, Beersheba is a modern city built at the edge of the desert on a site rich in history and biblical references. Considered by archaeologists to be one of the oldest human settlements in the country, Beersheba is often mentioned in the Hebrew scriptures. The name means "the well of the oath," referring to treaty sworn over the well dug by Abraham by the Patriarch and Abimelech king of Gerar, in which they promised not to "deal falsely" with each other (Gen. 21:23-23). The prophet Elijah sojourned in this region; Isaac, Jacob and Joshua passed through it; the people of Israel settled here after their return from Babylonia and Egypt. In the centuries that followed, Beersheba was nothing but a modest village at the gates of the desert. It became somewhat more important only at the end of the 19th century, when Turkish authorities attempted to transform it into an administrative center with control over the southern territories of Palestine.

After the English conquest of 1917, the small urban settlement seemed forgotten until the 1948 Arab-Israeli War, when it was contended by Egyptians and Israelis. Israel finally managed to secure the region. Since then, Beersheba has developed rapidly and is now one of the most vital cities in the country, complete with up-to-date tourist facilities and all the infrastructures of a large urban center. Besides an active industrial district which provides work for inhabitants throughout the region, the present capital of the Negev is also the home of numerous art centers, schools of all kinds, the prestigious **Ben Gurion University**, and a fine **museum** housed in the Old City's mosque. The dominant characteristic of today's Beersheba is undoubtedly its cosmopolitan flair: the city is inhabited by people from more than 70 countries. Many Bedouin live in a number of neighboring satellite towns or in traditional nomadic style in the Negev. The weekly Thursday-morning **Bedouin market** is one of the principal tourist attractions of the city, offering fine carpets, cushions, camel saddles, typical Arab headdresses, finely-worked furnishings, and many other examples of Bedouin handicrafts for sale.

The wild beauty of the southern Negev.

The ruins of a home at the Beersheba archaeological site.

The ruins of the "south church" at Shivta.

SHIVTA

Included in the UNESCO World Heritage Site list in 2005, the city of Shivta was founded by the Nabateans in the 2nd century BCE. But the majority of the ruins date to Byzantine times, when the city enjoyed a period of great prosperity. Three *churches* date to this period; also of considerable interest are the remains of the city's water supply system.

MAMSHIT

Not far from the town of Dimona, which is predominantly of French-speaking, North African origin, are the ruins of ancient Mamshit. This Nabatean settlement dates to the first century CE; archaeologists have uncovered the remains of two splendid Byzantine **churches** as well as impressive – and still remarkably well-preserved – water management systems from the Nabatean period. Many streets, several tombs, a cistern, a guard tower, and several-storied homes, including the so-called *House of the Affluent*, are all from the Nabatean period. Since 2005 the Mamshit archaeological site is under the tutelage of the UNESCO World Heritage program.

AVDAT

The ruins of Avdat perch in solitary splendor atop a hill that dominates the scorching desert plain. Avdat was an ancient Nabatean city dating to the third century BCE, which together with Mamshit, Haluza, Shivta, and Nizzana comprised the Nabatean Pentapolis. The Nabateans considered themselves descendants of Nebaioth, the eldest son of Ishmael, whose parents were Abraham and his concubine Hagar. Nabatean culture reached its zenith between the first century BCE and the early first century CE. Their wealth was considerable, since they effectively controlled the caravan routes leading from the Persian Gulf and Yemen to Damascus and Gaza. Avdat was a major station on the important road that linked Petra, the Nabatean capital, to Eilat and Gaza; it was a prosperous trade center when the Roman Emperor Trajan conquered the Negev in 106 CE. Excavations begun in 1952 have revealed many ruins, including two churches and a bath from the Byzantine period. It seems a mystery that ancient Avdat, surrounded by desert, was a productive agricultural settlement, but it appears that the Nabateans were masters in the art of "harvesting water"

Top, the remains of a Nabatean-era palace at Mamshit.
Left, the ruins of the ancient settlement of Avdat.

as it fell on the impermeable surface of the surrounding hills. Their ancient skill is now being imitated by modern settlers in the region.

TIMNA

The first copper mines in the world (worked at least 6000 years ago) were located at Timna, along the road that leads to Eilat and the Red Sea, as testified by the *excavations* and extensive studies carried out between 1959 and 1969 under the direction of Beno Rothenberg. According to tradition, the valley was the site of King Solomon's fabulous mines, where multitudes of slaves mined and smelted the ductile metal. It again became a mining center of considerable importance for copper and manganese in the early days of the State of Israel; a by-product of the mining enterprise is the beautiful teal-to-turquoise rock known as Eilat stone, which is an Israeli jewelry trademark.

A natural arch in the Timna Valley and the rock formation known as "Solomon's Pillars."

EILAT

At the southernmost tip of Israel, Eilat is the country's gateway to the Red Sea. It is located on the site of the ancient port, *Ezion-Geber*, another site contested since time immemorial by various peoples hoping to gain a seaport. According to tradition, Eilat is where King Solomon built ships and whence Hiram, king of Tyre, sent his men, "sailors who knew the sea," to serve in the fleet. (I Kings 9:26-28), but future-looking Eilat preserves very little of its millennia of history. It is an attractive seaside resort which promotes tourism and business. The port is of supreme importance, because it is Israel's only outlet to the Indian and Pacific Oceans; tons of merchandise are loaded and unloaded every day. The port has stimulated rapid development and immigration, the creation of new industries, and the implementation of great projects such as desalination of sea water for civil use, with the ultimate aim of reinforcing communications and transforming this ancient maritime center into an all-round modern seaside city. Prior to 1949, the lone outpost of Eilat was already a tourist paradise of international fame, where sun always shines, reflected by a crystal sea full of flamboyantly colored fish and corals. The sea world is now much more accessible, through the enormous portholes of the **Underwater Observatory**.

A panoramic view of Eilat, one of Israel's premier vacation spots.

*Top, one of the many species of fish that can be
seen at the Underwater Observatory.*

Left, the Underwater Observatory.

The highlands around Eilat.

Terraced hillside outside of Jerusalem.

INDEX